START & BUILD A SUCCESSFUL BUSINESS!

Your Guide to Becoming Your Own Boss, Achieving Prosperity, and Life-Changing Opportunities in 10 Simple Chapters, with Checklists, Real-Life Examples, Shortcuts, and Strategies for Success.

YOUR GUIDE TO PURPOSE, PROSPERITY & FREEDOM!

STEPHEN BROWN

START & BUILD A SUCCESSFUL BUSINESS!

YOUR GUIDE TO BECOMING YOUR OWN BOSS, ACHIEVING PROSPERITY, AND LIFE-CHANGING OPPORTUNITIES IN 10 SIMPLE CHAPTERS, WITH CHECKLISTS, REAL-LIFE EXAMPLES, SHORTCUTS, AND STRATEGIES FOR SUCCESS.

STEPHEN BROWN

CONTENTS

This book is dedicated to my parents, who always believed in me and gave me the desire to prove them right, and to those who didn't, who gave me the desire to prove them wrong!

My deepest thanks to all those who have helped and supported me on my business journey, without whom this book would not be written!

"A journey of a thousand miles begins with a single step."

LAO TSU.

INTRODUCTION

When I was 12, I had my first taste of entrepreneurship.

In the small Derbyshire village in England where I lived, all the houses had open fires. Early one morning, while on my daily newspaper delivery round, I came across an elderly lady I delivered newspapers to who was chopping sticks to light her fire. I stopped and helped, thinking little more of it, until my father, a self-employed landscape gardener, asked me to help him remove an old fence for one of his customers. At the suggestion of a bonfire to get rid of the scrap wood, I had an idea to take it home, break it up, and sell it in bundles as fire-starting sticks. My parents let me cover our small back garden with unsightly old fence panels. I then spent many hours over several weeks breaking up the old fencing and tying the wood into small bundles, which I would take with me on my newspaper round to sell.

Breaking up fence panels in the rain isn't most 12-year-old kids' idea of fun, nor was it mine. But by the time I'd finished, I'd established a base of loyal customers and bought a brand-new bike of my dreams, all paid for by my first business venture.

This early taste of entrepreneurship must have sown a seed as I went on to focus my studies and working life on the world of business, which today enables me to live with purpose, financial freedom, and time to enjoy the things in life that are important to me.

Now, don't get me wrong, I've since experienced lots of times, which felt a lot worse than breaking up fence panels in the cold winter rain, but starting and running a business reshaped my life and has provided me with three things that I value greatly:

1. Freedom to be my own boss with control over my own destiny.
2. Lifestyle and financial benefits beyond those available to me through employment.
3. Being of service to others.

Although my 12-year-old mind didn't fully understand business theory, much of this early experience is applicable to all businesses.

Starting a business can feel quite daunting; we've all heard about the big success stories and business personalities, which, whilst inspiring, can also be intimidating at the same time. If that's what you want to become, I hope this book is your first step. However, you don't need your business to turn you into a household name for it to provide you with the life and lifestyle you dream about.

Whatever your motivation, I've written this book as a no-nonsense guide and step-by-step manual for those who feel ready to reshape their life and start their first business. The idea of starting can feel overwhelming. That's why I've packed this book with practical guidance and, hopefully, a healthy mix of pragmatism and motivation. It's for aspiring entrepreneurs who need a clear path to follow without the fluff.

A bit about myself: I've always been passionate about serving others and building value. As a kid, I sold firewood, and later, as a college student, I funded my studies by selling handmade boxer shorts made from off-cut materials by my art student friend. I also gained my first taste of a service that would return to reshape my life when I helped my friends secure their industrial placements after I'd secured my own.

I started my first real business in a spare bedroom at home, which has since evolved into a multi-million-pound group of professional service companies.

At 23, I realised working for someone else wasn't for me! That realisation kick-started my first real business, which I've successfully run for over 30 years. Alongside this, I've had the privilege of studying and subsequently speaking at leading university business schools and business clubs in the UK and the USA, mentoring women in business across the world through The Cherie Blair Foundation, launching apps, helping charities to raise essential funds, advising businesses as a Non-Executive Director, and coaching many start-ups and early-stage companies.

So, why should this book matter to you?

With so much information out there, it can be difficult to find real-world advice that is also practical and joined-up. Many aspiring entrepreneurs find themselves lost in theory while searching for a solution. This book aims to fill that gap, providing processes, checklists, motivational stories, and key considerations to help you navigate the often-confusing path of starting a business. These are the things I wish I had at my fingertips when I started, which have since cost me tens of thousands of pounds and as many hours to learn and put into practice. The best of which I am now delighted to share with you.

This book is for you if you're motivated by financial freedom, the autonomy of running your own business, serving others, or creating your unique legacy. You may have a brilliant idea, but you're unsure of the first steps. This book will guide you through that initial stage, offering insights and practical advice. You may have already started your first business but have floundered in a specific area. If so, I've also designed this book to help you regroup and continue your business journey, better equipped to keep going.

Now, let's talk structure. I've crafted each chapter to provide a relevant real-world example, a motivational quote to inspire you, and a section dedicated to avoiding pitfalls.

Use this book as your toolkit and mentor to overcome fears and realise your business dreams. You have the passion. You have the drive. What you need now is guidance. And that's what this book aims to provide.

Written logically, I've outlined the steps you'll need to take to start your first business. You can also refer to specific chapters as needed for guidance on particular topics.

The key takeaway here is simple: All entrepreneurs are human, and we've all made mistakes along the way; by learning from the successes and mistakes of others, you will be better equipped to take your own first steps on this journey.

So, let's get started. The world is waiting for your business, your ideas, and your unique approach. Let's make it happen together.

CHAPTER 1
YOU AND YOUR IDEA!

BEFORE WE DELVE into the details of starting a business, it's essential to understand yourself and your motivations.

Starting a business is like starting a family; you can't walk away from your responsibilities, and it is potentially a lifelong commitment.

QUIZ: WHY DO YOU WANT TO START YOUR OWN BUSINESS?

Take this quick quiz to find out what's driving you!

For each statement, mark:

A – Strongly Agree
B – Agree
C – Neutral
D – Disagree
E – Strongly Disagree

- I want to have control over my time and how I work.
- I am motivated by building something that is my own.
- I'm looking for a way to earn more than I could as an employee.

- I often come up with ideas that I believe could solve real problems.
- I feel unfulfilled in my current job or career path.
- I want to create a lifestyle that aligns better with my values.
- I am excited about the challenges of entrepreneurship.
- I view business ownership as a means to positively impact my community and industry.
- I crave the freedom to make my own decisions without needing permission.
- I have a strong passion or skill that I can turn into a business.

If you answered mostly **A** or **B**:

You have strong internal motivation, with freedom, creativity, impact, and ownership being key drivers for you.

If you answered mostly **C**:

You may be curious but need clarity on your "why" before diving into business ownership.

If you answered mostly **D** or **E**:

You may be drawn to entrepreneurship for external reasons, such as dissatisfaction elsewhere, rather than a genuine passion; awareness will help you move forward more intentionally.

Based on your answers, write down why you are considering starting a business in one sentence. Keep this sentence close, as it will serve as your personal north star as you navigate this guide.

YOUR PERSONAL VISION BOARD:

A personal vision board is one of the most straightforward yet most powerful tools an aspiring entrepreneur can create. It's a visual representation of your dreams, goals, and the life you want to build, a constant reminder of *why* you are taking the risk to start your own business.

Creating a vision board is simple: bring together a collage of images, goal statements, and motivational quotes that represent your ambitions and arrange them on a page where you will constantly see them. Whether it's a thriving storefront, financial freedom, a global brand, or simply the lifestyle you envision, each element you place should spark motivation and inspiration.

More than just art, a vision board programs your subconscious mind to stay focused. When challenges inevitably arise, it serves as a compass, reminding you that today's struggles are stepping stones toward tomorrow's success. Over time, what starts as a collage of hope becomes a roadmap of action, fuelling persistence, creativity, and clarity.

In short, don't just plan your life; *see it*. A personal vision board makes your goals real long before they materialise.

I have mine as a screensaver, so I see it daily to keep me on track and focused.

UNDERSTANDING YOUR ENTREPRENEURIAL MINDSET

Starting your own business can feel like standing at the edge of a vast ocean. The waves crash at your feet, and the horizon stretches endlessly, promising adventure and uncertainty. You might ask yourself, "Do I have what it takes to succeed?"

If so, you are not alone. However, I also recall that the more time I spent acting rather than questioning myself, the more opportunities opened to me, the more evidence I collected for steering my business, the more successful I became. Action is better than inaction; even if you start in the wrong direction, at least you have momentum. Just try to find your bearings as quickly as possible!

To succeed as an entrepreneur, you must recognise certain psychological traits within yourself. Being opportunistic, resilient, adaptable, and risk-tolerant are the pillars of a strong entrepreneurial mindset. These traits aren't innate; they are more like muscles that get stronger with exercise.

Being opportunistic means being able to spot and seize opportunities that others may miss or overlook. You don't have to be an inventor with a new idea or a revolutionary vision. Most successful businesses spotted an undersupplied niche, identified a problem they could solve better, or felt they could offer a better service than what was currently on offer.

There are businesses everywhere, each serving their customers to a greater or lesser extent. Please take a moment to consider what you have purchased recently and the businesses behind them, including their processes, models, and structures.

Consider the infrastructure you currently have around you and the myriad of small businesses that came together to create it. Businesses and business owners are generating income from nearly everything you can see.

Recognising trends is also essential to being opportunistic, such as a growing sector of the economy, where there is room for you to offer a business with your own take on something.

Your opportunities don't have to be glamorous either; some of the most profitable businesses I know do the most mundane things, but critically, they either do them:

    a. better than the competition
    b. cheaper than the competition
    c. differently from the competition

In the early life example of my firewood business, my customers all burned coal on their fires, but my competition wasn't coal, which was cheap and abundant at the time. I also only had a bike so that I couldn't compete with coal merchants and their trucks anyway! The niche I spotted was a way to light the coal with dry sticks and, more specifically, a market segment of older people who found chopping wood difficult. Coal, wood, and fire had been around for a few million years; I saw a niche market. I had a supply of raw materials, which I spent my time adding value to by chopping, drying, and delivering to a customer base sufficiently near enough to service.

More often than not, your business opportunity involves something you already do for someone else, or perhaps a product or service you currently buy, where you notice certain shortcomings.

In 1996, I pivoted my then-marketing business, which specialised in the engineering sector, into an engineering recruitment business. I did this because my customers continuously told me they struggled to find engineers, and they alerted me to the underperformance of recruitment businesses in this sector. Recruitment was also the fastest-growing sector of the economy at the time, and my customers had provided me with the knowledge of what they wanted done differently.

Resilience is your ability to bounce back from setbacks. Imagine a rubber band; no matter how much you stretch it, it returns to its original shape. Successful entrepreneurs share this trait, facing obstacles but rising again, learning from each failure.

All successful entrepreneurs will have experienced a variety of failures. Such was the turbulent nature of my early business; I printed out and stuck on my office wall the following Sumo Wrestler saying:

"Success is only achieved by getting up one more time than you are knocked down!"

Adaptability is equally essential. Change is constant in today's fast-paced market, and those who can pivot find success. Think of adaptability as adjusting your sails according to the wind's direction. Risk tolerance is not about being reckless but having the courage to step into the unknown, weighing potential rewards against possible losses.

IT'S NOT ALL PLAIN SAILING!

You must also recognise that running your own business means you continuously risk your capital, time, and reputation. No large corporation can shield you or provide you with the same level of employee rights.

Have you ever seen the fairground act of plate spinning?

Running a business is often likened to spinning plates because it involves managing multiple tasks and responsibilities simultaneously, ensuring that each aspect of the business is functioning smoothly without neglecting any part.

Balancing Multiple Responsibilities: Just like a performer who spins multiple plates simultaneously, you must juggle various roles and tasks as a business owner. These include marketing, sales, finance, operations, customer service, and more. Each task requires attention and care to keep it "spinning" effectively.

Plate spinning requires constant attention to prevent them from falling. Similarly, running a business demands continuous monitoring and management. Neglecting any area, even briefly, can lead to problems that may affect the business's overall performance. Running a business also requires skill, energy, focus, and an eye for calculated risk.

And whilst we're at the fairground!

To quote an early mentor of mine:

"Running your own business is like a roller coaster ride, except the highs and lows are greater!"

OVERCOMING THE FEAR OF FAILURE

Fear of failure is an almost universal experience for entrepreneurs. At its core, fear is a natural response deeply rooted in our psychology, designed to protect us from danger. This instinct translates into a fear of financial loss, humiliation, or the unknown for entrepreneurs.

Yet, understanding this fear as a natural response to risk can be liberating. By acknowledging it, you can take steps to manage it effectively. Treat fear as a companion on your journey; it's allowed to ride with you but has no say in what snacks you take along, where the stops are, or what music you listen to!

Fear of failure also has an upside; it can be a strong motivator, and many entrepreneurs cite this as the key reason for their business success.

Managing your fear requires intentional strategies. Visualisation techniques can be powerful. Imagine yourself succeeding, vividly picture your steps to get there, and feel the emotions tied to that success. This practice rewires your brain to focus on positive outcomes, reducing anxiety about potential failures.

START WITH THE END IN MIND!

Write yourself a letter from the future. Imagine opening this letter to yourself five years from now; what would it say you have achieved? How does your business look and feel? How do you feel? What is your life like now? Where are you sitting? Who is with you? Who has helped you? Who have you helped?

The more vivid and colourful you can describe your future situation, the more likely you are to achieve the vision.

If you want to change your situation, another excellent technique is to draw a picture of how life currently looks and feels to you and then draw a picture of what you'd like it to look like.

These powerful visual representations of your thoughts enable you to understand your present and plan for the future.

Another helpful method is cognitive restructuring, which involves challenging and changing negative thought patterns. When faced with a daunting task, notice the automatic negative thoughts that arise and consciously reframe them into positive or neutral ones. Instead of thinking, "I'll never succeed," shift to, "I have the tools and determination to find a way forward."

IF AT FIRST YOU DON'T SUCCEED!

"Polite, Persistence Pays!"

The three P's, as they are known, are critical to every successful entrepreneur.

Many renowned entrepreneurs have faced significant setbacks but turned them into opportunities. Take J.K. Rowling, for instance. Before Harry Potter became a household name, multiple publishers rejected her manuscript. Her persistence and belief in her story eventually led to one of the most successful book series of all time. Her journey exemplifies the power of perseverance and seeing failure as a stepping stone rather than a stumbling block.

Another example is James Dyson, who created 5,126 failed prototypes before perfecting his revolutionary vacuum cleaner.

His story shows perseverance, and learning from each attempt can lead to remarkable success.

Or, consider Thomas Edison's journey with the light bulb. He famously said that he didn't fail 10,000 times, but instead found 10,000 ways that didn't work. His persistence and growth mindset led to one of the greatest inventions in history.

Building confidence comes from recognising and celebrating small wins along the way.

Setting micro-goals is an effective strategy for achieving your larger objectives. These are small, manageable tasks that contribute to your larger objectives. Completing them provides a sense of accomplishment and builds momentum.

For instance, if you want to launch a new product, start by setting daily tasks, such as researching packaging options or drafting social media posts. Each completed task is a victory that propels you forward.

Celebrating these small successes reinforces positivity and motivates continued effort. It's like training for a marathon; each completed run boosts your confidence and prepares you for the bigger challenge ahead. This approach builds skill and strengthens your belief in your abilities.

A practical exercise to help manage fear is creating a "failure resume." List past failures or setbacks, and beside each one, note what you learned and how it contributed to your growth.

This exercise can shift your perspective on failure from something to avoid to something valuable.

Consider the example of Apple's early struggles with products like the Newton PDA, a device that failed commercially but paved the way for later successes, such as the iPad and iPhone.

Apple's ability to learn from its failures and apply those lessons to future innovations highlights how overcoming fear and embracing failure can lead to ground-breaking success.

Also, consider this question:

"What is the worst thing that can happen?"

I know a doctor who identified an opportunity to establish a private health scanning service. He had compelling data, driven by the high number of requests for private health scans and the limited resources available to conduct them.

Fearful of stepping away from his well-paid job (which he needed for his lifestyle) and his concerns about his personal reputation if it failed, he asked himself, "What's the worst that can happen?" He realised that if it all failed, he could go back to being a doctor, and he would know that he had at least attempted to follow his dream of starting his own business.

I am pleased to say the story has a happy ending. He built a chain of private health scanning clinics, which he has since sold, and he is now enjoying a comfortable retirement. He may have failed and still be working for the British National Health Service, but he probably would still be anyway if he hadn't tried!

I share this story because many aspiring business owners fear leaving a comfortable, well-paid job, and the more you have to lose, the more difficult the decision becomes.

Personally, I never felt working for someone else would provide me with sufficient control over my own career. By starting and running my own business I have never had to worry about a restructuring or redundancy programme, and always felt far more secure relying on myself.

DISTRACTION AND LACK OF ACCOUNTABILITY: THE INVISIBLE KILLERS OF NEW BUSINESSES

When people imagine starting a business, they often think the main obstacles will be money, strategy, or competition. However, the most significant threats are usually internal: distraction and lack of accountability. These are the silent killers, and if you don't recognise and address them early, they can slowly erode your motivation, clarity, and momentum until your business stalls or never even launches.

DISTRACTION: THE SYSTEMATIC EROSION OF FOCUS

At its core, entrepreneurship demands prolonged, focused efforts to resolve complex problems. Strategic planning, product development, brand building, market penetration, customer acquisition, and service require your undivided attention and periods of deep, undisturbed work.

However, in today's environment, attention has become a commodity that is actively targeted by billion-dollar industries designed to exploit psychological weaknesses. Social media, streaming content, and messaging platforms are designed to fracture concentration and substitute short-term gratification for long-term achievement.

For entrepreneurs, the stakes of distraction are far higher than for the average individual. Every diverted hour delays product launches, dilutes marketing efforts, weakens strategic planning, and compromises competitiveness.

Key manifestations of entrepreneurial distraction include:

- **Chronic task-switching** leads to cognitive fatigue and diminished output quality.
- **Prioritising trivial tasks** (e.g., logo refinement, endless

website tweaks) over critical growth activities (sales, customer discovery, market testing).

- **Overconsumption of information** under the guise of "research" results in paralysis rather than action.

Unchecked, distraction doesn't merely slow a business; it can end it!

LACK OF ACCOUNTABILITY: FREEDOM WITHOUT DISCIPLINE

When I left employment to start my first business, the owner, a very successful Irish business tycoon, gave me a lasting piece of advice:

"Most people who start their own business like the idea of not having a boss; however, when you have a business, all your customers are your boss!"

Entrepreneurship is often romanticised as ultimate freedom: no boss, time clock, or corporate bureaucracy. But freedom without structure is not liberty; it is chaos. In traditional employment, accountability systems, like managers, performance evaluations, and deadlines, create external pressures that drive productivity. In entrepreneurship, those systems vanish. Without the proactive creation of accountability mechanisms, progress becomes optional.

Common symptoms of accountability failure among entrepreneurs include:

- Slippage of deadlines without consequence or adjustment.
- Avoiding uncomfortable tasks (e.g., cold outreach, financial planning) in favour of busywork.

- Lack of measurable objectives, leading to unfocused daily activity.
- Rationalisation of poor performance ("I'm just waiting for the right time," "The market isn't ready yet").

Without accountability, entrepreneurs drift into patterns of self-deception, mistaking activity for achievement and movement for progress.

It is not the difficulty of entrepreneurship that defeats most first-time founders; it is the lack of discipline to impose their own standards and hold themselves to them rigorously.

ESTABLISHING SYSTEMS TO COMBAT DISTRACTION AND ENFORCE ACCOUNTABILITY

Recognising these threats is not enough. Entrepreneurs must construct formal systems designed to counteract natural human tendencies.

Strategic Environment Design

Entrepreneurs must engineer their work environment to minimise external stimuli that fragment attention.

- Create an uncluttered workspace used solely for focused work.
- Delete or block non-essential apps and websites during work hours.
- Schedule blocks of time for deep work.
- Swallow the Frog! Conquer your day by tackling the hardest task first:

One of the simplest but most effective productivity strategies for entrepreneurs is known as "Swallow the Frog First." The idea comes from Brian Tracy's bestselling book *Eat That Frog!* (2001), which draws on a quote often attributed to Mark Twain:

> "If it's your job to eat a frog, it's best to do it first thing in the morning."

In this metaphor, the "frog" represents your most difficult, important, or procrastination-prone task, the one that makes you groan just thinking about it, but that will also have the most significant impact on your progress.

As a new entrepreneur, your day will fill up quickly with emails, small wins, and distractions. However, if you begin your day by "swallowing the frog", completing your hardest or highest-value task first, you gain momentum, clarity, and a sense of control. It prevents you from being busy without being productive.

- Identify your "frog" the night before. Choose one task that, if completed, would make the day a success.
  - Do it first thing in the morning. Avoid checking email or diving into more manageable tasks beforehand.
  - Repeat daily. Making this a habit builds discipline and focus, critical skills for any entrepreneur.

Successful founders don't avoid discomfort; they face it head-on. Swallow the frog, and the rest of your day will go down a whole lot smoother.

There is also real science behind this principle; tackling a challenging task first thing in the morning boosts productivity and helps regulate your brain's dopamine, the chemical linked to motivation and reward. When you avoid easy wins, such as checking your phone, and instead focus on something challenging but meaningful, you trigger a healthier, more sustainable dopamine response. You will find that your focus improves for the rest of the day, and your brain associates effort with long-term satisfaction, a powerful habit for any entrepreneur.

PRECISION GOAL SETTING AND TRACKING

Goals must be specific, time-bound, and measurable. Vague ambitions, such as "grow the business," are replaced with precise targets, like "secure five paying clients by the end of Q2." What gets measured improves, and what gets measured and reported upon improves exponentially.

Entrepreneurs must introduce accountability into their professional lives intentionally; mechanisms to do this include:

- Working with an accountability partner who is authorised to challenge and critique progress.
- Joining a mastermind group of serious entrepreneurs who set goals and meet at defined intervals to provide structured feedback.
- Making explicit promises regarding launches, product releases, or milestones to stakeholders, customers, or communities.

External visibility and social pressure must fill the gap where natural discipline is insufficient.

A disciplined entrepreneur conducts a weekly review that asks hard, unflinching questions:

- Did I honour my time blocks?
- What critical actions did I complete?
- What did I avoid, and why?
- What specific outcomes moved the business forward?
- What must be corrected immediately?

Those who learn to fight and win on this inner battlefield give themselves a decisive advantage over the majority who will quietly surrender!

SELF-AUDIT FOR ENTREPRENEURIAL READINESS

If you continue reading this book, you still have the desire, drive, and will feel equipped to start your first business.

It's now essential for you to check that your business aligns with your competencies, knowledge, skills, and personal values.

If you still think it's for you, then give yourself the choice!

Next, assess your readiness for entrepreneurship. Here's an exercise to help you evaluate your entrepreneurial mindset:

Take a moment to reflect on your personal strengths and weaknesses. What are your natural talents? Where do you excel? Conversely, what are areas where you struggle? Write them down. This exercise helps you understand where you stand and what you must work on.

Are you in the right business?

There are four main types of business:

- **Experience-based business:** You take what you currently do as your job and do it for customers yourself.
- **Passion-based business:** You take your passion or hobby and do it for a living.
- **Idea-based business:** You bring an idea for a product or service to market.
- **Competency-based business:** You use your natural capabilities to add value and serve customers.

There are positives and negatives for all the main types of new business. Here are a few to consider:

Experience-Based Business

Positives: Established Expertise: You already possess the necessary skills and knowledge.
Existing Network: You can leverage professional contacts.
Lower Learning Curve: Familiarity with industry standards and practices.
Credibility: Easier to gain trust from clients and stakeholders.
Negatives: Limited Innovation: May stick to conventional methods.
Burnout Risk: Continuing the same work can lead to fatigue.
Market Saturation: Competing with established businesses.
Dependency on Previous Employer: Potential conflicts or non-compete clauses.

Passion-Based Business

Positives:
High Motivation: Passion drives commitment and resilience.
Personal Fulfilment: Enjoyment in daily work.
Strong Brand Identity: Authenticity attracts loyal customers.
Negatives:
Skill Gaps: Passion doesn't always equate to expertise.
Market Demand: Passion projects may not have a large market.
Financial Risk: Emotional attachment can cloud judgment.
Work-Life Balance: Blurring the Lines Between Hobby and Business.

Idea-Based Business

Positives:
Innovation: Potential to disrupt markets with new solutions.
Scalability: Unique ideas can attract investors and grow rapidly.
Competitive Edge: Differentiation from existing products/services.
Intellectual Property: The possibility to patent and protect ideas.
Negatives:
High Uncertainty: The risk that an idea may not be viable.
Resource-intensive: Requires a significant investment in R&D.
Market Education: Need to educate consumers about new concepts.
Execution Challenges: Turning Ideas into Practical Solutions.

Competency-Based Business

Positives:
Natural Strengths: Leveraging inherent skills and talents.
Adaptability: Ability to pivot and adjust based on strengths.
Customer Value: High-quality service/product due to competency.
Personal Satisfaction: Working within your comfort zone.
Negatives:
Skill Limitations: You may need to develop additional skills.
Market Fit: Competencies may not align with market needs.
Growth Constraints: Scaling can be challenging without a diverse set of skills.
Overconfidence: Risk of underestimating business complexities.

If you have the benefit of combining more than one of the above, you increase your chances of success.

When I started my recruitment business, I had no experience running a business of this nature, which was beneficial, as I'd have started with too many limiting beliefs. What I did have was a strong competency in communication, and I was finally able to put my talkative personality to good use!

Growing up, my passion, however, was nature. Thankfully, I ignored my school career advisor's suggestion of becoming a Nature Reserve Warden, although it was a subject I care about, it wasn't an area where I had any demonstrable competency, and I didn't feel that my relaxing outlet would be sufficiently challenging or rewarding as a career. I now get to enjoy nature on my own terms, when I want to, and without it feeling like a job. I now also have the additional bonus of a business, which I am equally passionate about, and the positive impact I can make with it.

ALIGNING PERSONAL VALUES WITH BUSINESS GOALS

Start by brainstorming your core values; what truly matters to you? Is it innovation, community impact, creating a better life for you and your family, freedom from corporate life, financial independence, creating the best product, or delivering the best service? Once you have identified these values, draft a mission statement that encapsulates them alongside your business aspirations.

For instance, if environmental sustainability is crucial to you, ensure your business practices align with this value. Perhaps your mission statement could be: "To develop innovative products that enhance everyday life while preserving our planet for future generations."

Look at Patagonia as an exemplar, a company driven by environmental sustainability at its core. Every decision reflects its mission to protect nature while providing quality outdoor gear.

Or, on a smaller scale but by no means of any less importance, is a craft brewery located in Devon, which has embraced sustainability from the outset, using solar power and a natural water spring to power their operations.

By understanding your mindset and aligning your values with your goals, you're better equipped to face the challenges of entrepreneurship. As we explore further chapters, remember these foundational lessons in resilience, adaptability, growth mindset cultivation, and value alignment will guide every step of your entrepreneurial journey.

ENTREPRENEURIAL READINESS CHECKLIST

Use this checklist to assess your readiness for starting and operating a business. Check each statement that applies to you.

Personal Traits and Skills:

1. **Passion and Commitment**
   - I am deeply passionate about my business idea and its potential impact.
   - I am willing to dedicate significant time, effort, and resources to my business, even during challenging times.
2. **Risk Tolerance**
   - I am comfortable taking calculated risks and understand the potential consequences.
   - I can handle uncertainty and ambiguity without becoming overly stressed.
3. **Resilience and Perseverance**
   - I can bounce back from setbacks and failures, learning from them to improve my approach.
   - I am persistent in achieving my goals, even when faced with obstacles.
4. **Adaptability**
   - I can adapt to changing circumstances and pivot my business strategy when necessary.
   - I am open to new ideas, feedback, and continuous learning to improve my business.

5. **Decision-Making**
   - I can make decisions quickly and confidently, even with incomplete information.
   - I am comfortable taking responsibility for my decisions and their outcomes.

Business Skills and Knowledge:

1. **Market Understanding**
   - I thoroughly understand my target market, including demographics, preferences, and behaviours.
   - I have identified a clear need or problem that my business will address, and I understand the competitive landscape.
2. **Financial Literacy**
   - I understand basic financial principles, including budgeting, cash flow management, and financial forecasting.
   - I am comfortable with financial planning, including setting financial goals and tracking performance.
3. **Marketing and Sales**
   - I have a well-defined marketing strategy for promoting my products or services, encompassing digital marketing, social media, and traditional methods.
   - I am confident in my ability to effectively sell my products or services, having developed effective sales techniques.
4. **Operational Skills**
   - I understand the day-to-day operations required to run my business, including inventory management, supplier relationships, and logistics.
   - I have developed efficient processes and systems to ensure smooth operations and scalability.

5. **Leadership and Management**
    - I have experience leading and managing teams, including hiring, training, and motivating employees.
    - I can effectively delegate tasks and responsibilities, ensuring my team works collaboratively towards common goals.

Support and Resources:

1. **Network and Relationships**
    - I have a strong network of mentors, advisors, industry contacts, and potential partners who can provide valuable insights and support.
    - I am willing to seek help and advice when needed and actively invest time in building and maintaining relationships.
2. **Access to Capital & Cash**
    - I have a clear plan for funding my business, including personal savings, loans, investors, or other sources of capital.
    - I understand the financial requirements to start and sustain my business, as well as my personal financial commitments, and have contingency plans in place.
3. **Work-Life Balance**
    - I have considered how starting a business will impact my personal life and have strategies in place to maintain a healthy work-life balance.
    - I am prepared to manage the demands of entrepreneurship while ensuring my well-being and personal relationships are not neglected.

Self-Reflection:

1. **Motivation and Goals**
   - I have a clear vision and well-defined goals for my business, encompassing both short-term and long-term objectives.
   - I am motivated by more than just financial gain, such as a passion for the industry, a desire to make an impact, or personal fulfilment.
2. **Self-Awareness**
   - I am aware of my strengths and weaknesses, and I am committed to ongoing learning and self-improvement.
   - I regularly reflect on my performance and seek feedback to enhance my skills and business practices.

Reflection

- **Total Checks**: Count the number of statements you checked.
- **Analysis**: Reflect on the areas where you did not check the statements. These areas may require further development or attention before starting your entrepreneurial journey.

Use this checklist as a guide to assess and improve your readiness for entrepreneurship.

A high score indicates strong entrepreneurial readiness, while a lower score suggests areas for growth and development. Use this self-audit as a starting point to prepare yourself for the entrepreneurial journey and identify which aspects of this book you may need to focus on more closely.

Consider returning to this checklist once you have completed this book and reassess your confidence and readiness to start and build a successful business with your new found knowledge.

IDENTIFYING YOUR UNIQUE VALUE PROPOSITION

Once you have established your readiness and you have a business idea, you need to understand your unique value proposition (UVP). Your UVP serves as your beacon in the bustling business arena, explaining why customers should choose you over the competition.

Consider it the elevator pitch for your entire enterprise, summarising why your product or service is the best choice. It's not just about what you offer but how you solve a problem in a way that others don't. This clarity is vital, especially in crowded markets where differentiation is key.

Imagine you're at a farmers' market, surrounded by stalls selling similar produce. What makes your stall stand out? Is it the organic certification, the heirloom variety no one else has, or the sustainable packaging? Your UVP is the concise statement that captures this essence, ensuring your business doesn't get lost in the noise.

In most small businesses, the UVP and your brand are YOU!

People still buy from people, and your personality, responsiveness, and presence are why your customers choose you over your competitors. This can be why one restaurant has a waiting list for tables, while a neighbouring one stands empty.

Write down what you will offer that your customers want, which makes you different.

I was once with the CEO of a leading German car franchise when one of his Area Managers called to say he'd found the perfect location for their new site in a large city.

The CEO's reply:

"Great, now show me the people who will stand on it!"

He knew the importance of having the right people representing his business and the potential cost of having the wrong ones.

To craft a UVP that resonates, first assess market needs and gaps. You can start with thorough research. Tools like SWOT analysis (strengths, weaknesses, opportunities, and threats) are invaluable for understanding where the market lacks. Look for underserved segments, those niches that competitors have overlooked or failed to appreciate. For instance, if you're venturing into the tech industry, many companies focus on cutting-edge innovation, but perhaps there's a demand for user-friendly solutions that cater to tech-averse audiences.

Discovering these gaps is like finding hidden treasures; it requires patience and keen observation.

Once you've identified these opportunities, crafting a compelling UVP involves a step-by-step approach. Start by highlighting what makes your offering different. Map out your benefits against those of your competitors. Consider aspects like price, quality, service, and convenience. For example, if you're launching a food delivery service, your differentiator may be to offer locally sourced meals delivered in eco-friendly packaging. Your UVP might be: "Delivering fresh, local flavours straight to your door with zero carbon footprint." This statement is specific and speaks directly to eco-conscious consumers.

CRAFTING A COMPELLING UVP

To ensure your UVP hits the mark, draw inspiration from case studies of successful businesses. Take Apple, known for its seamless integration of hardware and software, a UVP that has set it apart for decades. Or consider Dollar Shave Club, which disrupted the razor market with an affordable subscription model and a cheeky brand voice.

Their UVP was clear: "A great shave for a few bucks a month." Such examples illustrate the power of a well-defined proposition that speaks directly to consumer needs and desires.

Testing and refining your UVP is an ongoing process. Please encourage customers to share their thoughts on your brand's strengths and weaknesses. This feedback is invaluable; use it to continually tweak and improve your UVP.

Test Market Questionnaires:

If your business is Business-to-Business (B2B), speaking directly with potential customers is the best place to start gathering information to include in your UVP, ideally by phone or in person.

Testing your market can also be a way of building a pipeline of potential sales leads for your business.

Whenever I launch a new business, service, or division, I create a "Test Market Questionnaire" to discuss with potential customers.

In it, I ask about their current use of that product or service, what they like about it, their suppliers, and what they would like done differently, after which I ask:

"If we developed a product or service that could meet these additional requirements, would you like to discuss it with us?"

Suppose your business is Business-to-Consumer (B2C). In that case, you can still use this method by meeting the people likely to buy your product or service and stopping and asking them, or if you have a big idea with a big market of consumers (and a bigger budget to match), you can have a professional market research survey done on your behalf.

Other ways to gauge your product or service's appeal include creating a web landing page with a registration form to capture interest. You can market this to your target audience through advertising or direct marketing to existing contacts, including via messages on networking platforms or social media. The goal is to determine how many potential customers express interest. Ask them no more than three questions about what interests them.

A/B TESTING

A/B testing is used when you have several ideas and want to determine which one receives the best response. It's like a contest between two ideas. You show one version (A) to some people and a different version (B) to others, and see which one performs better, such as which ad gets more clicks or which email gets more responses.

Use A/B testing whenever you're unsure which option will yield better results, such as when selecting a headline, a product photo, or a special offer.

It eliminates the guesswork from decisions. Instead of hoping you're right, you get real proof of what works best, helping your business grow faster and smarter.

Most established businesses continuously test and validate using this method to remain current and improve their service, product, messaging, and sales performance. They also incorporate customer feedback into regular reviews to spot new emerging trends.

Staying tuned to these changes makes sure your UVP remains relevant and compelling. For instance, if more customers are concerned about sustainability, your proposition might emphasise eco-friendly practices more prominently.

Real-world feedback is essential for you to refine your UVP. Consider the example of Burt's Bees, which began with home-made beeswax lip balms and expanded into a complete line of natural personal care products in response to consumer demand for natural ingredients. Their UVP evolved from simply "natural" to "earth-friendly natural personal care products," reflecting a more profound commitment to environmental stewardship as consumer consciousness grew.

Remember that crafting and refining your UVP is not set in stone. Business landscapes evolve, technologies advance, and consumer preferences shift, all requiring adaptation. Regularly revisit your proposition to ensure it aligns with both your business goals and market demands. Embrace flexibility and remain open to change; these are essential traits in the entrepreneurial toolkit.

Keep your UVP clear, concise, and focused on customer benefits rather than features. This focus ensures it remains impactful and memorable. A strong UVP communicates what you offer and why it matters to those you serve. Through careful evaluation of market needs, thoughtful crafting of your proposition, and ongoing refinement based on feedback, you'll build a solid foundation for business success that stands resilient amidst competition.

The process of developing a UVP is both strategic and creative. It requires an understanding of your market, an awareness of competitive dynamics, and a deep connection with customer needs. As you navigate this terrain, remember that your UVP is more than just marketing jargon; it's a promise to your customers about the value they can expect.

VALIDATING YOUR BUSINESS IDEA WITH REAL-WORLD FEEDBACK

Feedback from the real world is like a compass for your business idea, guiding you to stay on the right path. Early feedback is crucial as it provides insights that can shape and refine your concept before you dive headfirst into development. Think of it as having a conversation with your future customers. They tell you what they like, what they don't, and what could be improved. This invaluable input can save you time and resources, preventing missteps before they become costly.

When I started my first small business, I quickly learned the importance of listening. Customers would point out things I hadn't thought of, opening my eyes to new possibilities and ideas. This interaction isn't just about gathering opinions; it's about learning what truly matters to those you're trying to serve.

Gathering this feedback requires a thoughtful approach. Surveys and focus groups are excellent methods for collecting detailed information from potential customers. Surveys allow you to reach a broad audience quickly, capturing quantitative data that helps identify trends and preferences. Platforms like Survey-Monkey or Google Forms can be instrumental in this process. Focus groups, on the other hand, provide qualitative insights. By bringing together a small group of people, you can hold deeper discussions, uncovering nuances that surveys might miss. These sessions lend themselves well to understanding consumer behaviour.

One-on-one interviews offer another layer of depth, allowing for a more personal connection where potential users feel comfortable sharing honest feedback. You can ask specific questions about their needs and how they perceive your idea fitting into their lives. These conversations provide rich, detailed insights that are often more candid than those obtained through other methods. I remember hosting informal coffee meetups with potential customers while testing a new service idea. The relaxed environment encouraged open dialogue, and the feedback was invaluable.

Once you've collected this feedback, the next step is to iterate on your business idea. Iteration is an ongoing process of refining and improving based on what you've learned, leading to tweaking a product feature, rethinking your marketing approach, or even pivoting to a new product, service, or business model. There's a famous story about Instagram, launched initially as Burbn, a platform focusing on check-ins and social plans. User feedback showed that people were primarily interested in the photo-sharing feature. The founders listened and pivoted, and the rest is history.

Continuous improvement loops are about implementing changes, testing them, and seeking further feedback. This cycle ensures that your business evolves in response to real-world needs rather than assumptions. It's like fine-tuning an instrument; slight adjustments can lead to harmony.

MINIMUM VIABLE PRODUCT (MVP)

Building a Minimum Viable Product (MVP) is another powerful strategy in this process. An MVP allows you to test your business idea with minimal resources, focusing on core features that deliver value to early adopters. It's about creating a simplified version of your product to validate assumptions and gather user feedback quickly.

To create an MVP, start by identifying the most crucial functions of your product, those that directly solve the problem you're addressing. Strip away anything non-essential. This approach saves time and ensures you're focusing on what truly matters to users.

Consider Dropbox's MVP strategy: a simple video demonstrating how the service worked was enough to gauge interest and gather feedback without building the entire product up front. This example illustrates that an MVP doesn't always have to be a physical product; sometimes a demonstration or prototype suffices.

Testing your MVP with real users provides the insights needed to refine and improve before full-scale development. Collect feedback on usability, features, and overall satisfaction. Use this data to decide which aspects to enhance or modify.

As you work through these steps, remember that validation is not a one-time event but an integral part of your business development process. Continue to engage with your audience, adapt based on their needs, and remain open to change.

Incorporating real-world feedback into your business strategy is not only beneficial but also necessary for sustainable success. By actively listening to potential customers, iterating based on their input, and testing ideas with an MVP, you position yourself to create a product or service that genuinely resonates with your target market.

As you move forward with your business idea, let this feedback-driven approach guide you toward innovation that meets real needs and creates a lasting impact.

PUTTING YOUR TOE IN THE WATER:

In his book *"Great by Choice,"* Jim Collins decodes what makes businesses successful. He employs the term "calibrated bullets," a concept that is particularly relevant in the context of how companies achieve greatness in environments of uncertainty and chaos.

The idea of calibrated bullets is part of Collins' broader framework for disciplined innovation and decision-making, especially in conditions of uncertainty.

Collins contrasts the approach of "calibrated bullets" with that of "flying by the seat of your pants" or taking reckless, high-risk leaps. The term refers to a disciplined, experimental approach to decision-making where a company (or individual) tests small, controlled, low-risk actions (the "bullets") before making larger, more impactful moves (the "cannonballs").

The strategy involves testing and refining ideas with small, manageable experiments before fully committing resources. This "calibration" process enables you to fine-tune your plan, learn from each test, and increase the chances of success when you eventually make a more significant decision or commitment.

Once there's enough confidence and data about what works, you can then make a bigger, more impactful decision (cannonball).

This approach is more strategic and less risky than jumping into large initiatives without understanding how they will unfold.

The key here is the calibration process. Just like a gun's sights can be adjusted to ensure accuracy, companies adjust their strategies through small, iterative steps that allow them to learn, improve, and adapt without committing too much to a single untested idea. It's a more educated, data-driven approach to risk-taking.

Another way to stack the odds in your favour before embarking upon your new venture is to conduct a PESTEL Analysis, a great way to identify any tailwinds or headwinds you will encounter. It also suggests whether the environment for your business provides longer-term opportunities to grow.

USING A PESTEL ANALYSIS TO TEST IF TRENDS ARE ON YOUR SIDE

PESTEL Analysis is a strategic tool used by businesses to scan and interpret the macro-environmental factors that can influence their operations, decisions, and long-term planning. The acronym stands for Political, Economic, Social, Technological, Environmental, and Legal; six broad categories that encompass everything from government policy to societal values and technological disruption. By systematically exploring each area, businesses can uncover potential opportunities and threats that lie outside their immediate control but may significantly shape their strategic direction.

For example, an increase in employment legislation could suggest opportunities for an HR Services business, a podcasting trend could provide the opportunity for a specialist media channel, or increased government spending on road maintenance could increase opportunities for a traffic management business.

CHAPTER 2
BUSINESS PLANNING ESSENTIALS

WHEN I LOOK BACK at starting my current company, one of the things I am most grateful for was the time I spent planning before it launched.

This had three main benefits:

- On day one, the business looked and felt like a bigger company (I even sent my first voice out as number 1001, so my first client didn't realise they were my first and only customer).
- By planning, I'd created a business model with vision, values, UVP, systems, and processes we could grow into.
- Once up and running, there was very little time to spend on planning, as I was consumed by doing!

The deeper you can lay these foundations, the stronger the business you build will be.

However, beware of using this step as an excuse to procrastinate. Set yourself a launch date and work to this deadline.

CRAFTING A VISION, VALUES AND MISSION FOR YOUR BUSINESS

Picture yourself standing on the threshold of your new venture, brimming with ideas yet seeking direction. This is where crafting a vision and mission for your business becomes vital. Think of your vision as the North Star by which you will navigate and guide your business to realise your long-term aspirations. While your mission serves as the compass, steering your daily operations. A vision statement captures your dreams, painting a vivid picture of what you hope to achieve in the future. Conversely, a mission statement grounds you in the present, focusing on the core purpose and values that drive your business forward.

I can't emphasise the importance of this statement enough. Despite several reviews, the one I wrote for Euro Projects Recruitment over 30 years ago is still the one we use today. It's a single sentence stating how we intend to present ourselves, to whom, and for what purpose.

"Making work meaningful by providing the most professional, friendly, and high-quality service to our clients and candidates alike."

Creating a powerful vision statement starts with brainstorming. Gather your thoughts and imagine the ideal future for your business. What impact do you wish to make? How do you envision your company in five, ten, or even twenty years? This exercise helps crystallise your goals into a single aspirational statement that inspires both you and your team. Consider examples from successful companies like Tesla, whose vision "to create the most compelling car company of the 21st century" communicates ambition and innovation. A well-crafted vision statement motivates and aligns everyone involved with your overarching objectives.

Now, let's talk about developing a concise mission statement. A strong mission statement communicates your business's purpose and values. It should be specific, capturing the essence of what you do and why you do it. Begin by listing key aspects of your business, your products or services, your target audience, and your unique approach. Then, distil these elements into a brief statement that resonates with authenticity.

Spending time defining your values is paramount to the success of your business; it defines your culture and therefore the rails on which your business will run. Initially, these values will most likely embody your own guiding morals and principles, as you scale and grow, they become the essential foundation for your vision, mission and culture.

Take, for instance, Patagonia's mission: "Build the best product, cause no unnecessary harm, use business to inspire and implement solutions to the environmental crisis." It's succinct yet meaningful, reflecting their commitment to quality and sustainability.

To help you craft your own mission statement, consider this checklist:

Mission Statement Checklist

- Identify core products or services.
- Define the target audience.
- Clarify the unique value proposition.
- Highlight values and principles.
- Keep it clear and concise.

Aligning your values, vision, and mission with daily operations is essential for maintaining focus and consistency. A set of values and a vision statement aren't just words on paper; they should be embedded in your company culture. Encourage employees to embody these ideals through their work, fostering a sense of purpose and unity. Strategies include incorporating values and vision into team meetings or celebrating achievements that bring you closer to realising them. For instance, if part of your values and vision involves sustainability, make eco-friendly practices an integral part of everyday decisions.

Similarly, incorporate your mission into operational decisions by using it as a guiding principle. When confronted with choices or challenges, refer to your mission to ensure it aligns with your foundational values. This approach helps maintain integrity while avoiding distractions that could impede progress.

Consider how Zappos exemplifies mission-driven decision-making. Their focus on delivering exceptional customer service is reflected in every aspect of their operations, from hiring practices that prioritise cultural fit to empowering employees to exceed expectations for customers. By weaving their values, vision, and mission into the fabric of their business, Zappos creates an environment where employees are motivated and customers feel valued.

The guiding principles of values, vision and mission will enable you to set and manage clear expectations for how your business is run, including:

- Who you decide to recruit for your team.
- Behaviours that you encourage, recognise, and reward, as well as those that you need to confront.
- Your approach to conducting business, whom it is for, and the intended purpose.
- The people you associate with: You are known by the company you keep.
- All critical decisions contribute to how your business is perceived, what it stands for, and your overall brand.

In conclusion, crafting a compelling set of values, vision, and mission is more than an exercise in branding; it is about setting the stage for success by providing clarity and direction. Through the thoughtful development of these statements and their intentional integration into daily operations, you will create a strong foundation upon which to build your business. This foundation inspires, guides, and propels you towards realising your entrepreneurial dreams.

SETTING SMART BUSINESS GOALS

You've got values, a vision and a mission; now it's time to get specific with SMART goals. This concept isn't just a catchy acronym; it's a framework that can guide you to tangible achievements. SMART stands for Specific, Measurable, Achievable, Relevant, and Time-bound. Each component plays a critical role in steering you toward success. Specificity means setting clear goals, so you know exactly what you're aiming for. Measurable goals let you track progress, ensuring you stay on course. Achievable keeps your ambitions grounded, while Relevant ensures they align with broader business objectives. Finally, being time-bound gives you a deadline, creating urgency and focus.

Imagine you're sitting at your desk, a notebook open with a pen poised over a blank page. It's time for a goal-setting workshop. Start with the specifics by asking yourself what exactly you want to achieve. Instead of saying, "I want more customers," specify, "I want to increase my customer base by 20%." Next, think about measurability. How will you know when you've reached that 20%? Maybe it's through weekly sales reports or monthly growth charts. Keep it realistic and achievable; setting a goal to double your customer base in a month might not be feasible. Relevance ties into your larger mission. Does this goal help fulfil your business purpose? Lastly, set a timeline. When do you want to hit this target? A deadline of six months gives you a practical timeframe.

Tracking progress is crucial; it's like having a map on a road trip. Project management tools like Trello or Asana can be lifesavers here, as they organise tasks and monitor advancements. They help create visual timelines and assign responsibilities, ensuring everyone knows what they need to do and by when. Regular goal review meetings also keep accountability in check. These gatherings aren't just about number crunching; they're opportunities to celebrate small victories and recalibrate if necessary. Imagine sitting down with your team, going over metrics, and discussing what's working and what's not. It's like fine-tuning an instrument to get the perfect pitch.

In all our businesses, we operate Kanban boards using Trello. "Kanban" is a Japanese word that means "signboard" or "visual signal." In the context of work and project management, it originated from Toyota's manufacturing system in the 1940s. They used physical cards (Kanbans) to signal steps in the production process, helping teams visualise work, limit waste, and improve efficiency.

Kanban boards are visual tools used to manage work by showing tasks as cards that move through columns like "To Do," "In Progress," and "Done." This simple layout helps you see what needs to be done, who's working on what, and where bottlenecks might be. It's an ideal system for first-time business owners to stay organised and focused without getting overwhelmed.

Trello is a popular online tool that brings the Kanban board to life digitally. It's easy to use, free to start, and allows you to drag and drop tasks, assign team members, set deadlines, and add checklists or attachments. Whether you're planning a product launch or tracking daily tasks, a Kanban system helps you stay on top of your business activities with clarity and flexibility. You also get a little hit of that miracle chemical dopamine when you move your project along the board, allowing small wins towards bigger goals.

Flexibility in goal setting is just as important as the goals themselves. The business landscape is ever-changing, and rigidity can be a downfall. Be prepared to adjust your goals as circumstances evolve. Perhaps midway through your plan, as new market research indicates a shift in consumer behaviour. This is where evaluating goal relevance comes into play. Are your goals still aligned with current market dynamics? If not, don't hesitate to pivot. Real-life examples abound; think of businesses that had to adapt during economic downturns or technological shifts yet thrived by being agile and responsive.

Consider a scenario where you set a goal that initially seemed perfect: launching a new product line by year-end. However, supply chain issues arise, causing delays. Instead of viewing this as a setback, could you reassess your timeline and adjust expectations accordingly? This adaptability can be the difference between falling short and ultimately succeeding. It's about staying focused on the destination while remaining open to changing paths if necessary.

Goal adaptation is not a sign of weakness but rather a strategic response to real-world challenges. It ensures that your business remains relevant and competitive, regardless of external circumstances. The ability to flexibly respond to changes can foster resilience within your team, encouraging them to view challenges as opportunities for growth rather than insurmountable obstacles.

In conclusion, setting SMART goals is not just about ticking boxes; it's about creating a roadmap that guides you toward achieving meaningful objectives. Through careful planning, diligent tracking, and adaptive flexibility, these goals become the stepping stones on your path to success. As you refine your approach to goal setting, remember that the journey is as important as the destination, offering invaluable lessons and insights along the way.

BUILDING A DYNAMIC BUSINESS MODEL CANVAS

Imagine trying to piece together a puzzle without knowing what the final picture looks like. That's what running a business can feel like without a clear model. Enter the Business Model Canvas, your strategic management tool, a blueprint that brings structure to an idea, laying out the essentials of your business on a single page. It's like having a map for all the crucial parts of your venture, from identifying key partners to understanding revenue streams. The canvas is divided into segments, each playing a pivotal role in outlining your business's architecture. Value propositions focus on what makes your product or service unique. Customer segments identify who you're serving. Channels outline how you reach your customers, while customer relationships define how you interact with them. Revenue streams highlight how you earn money, and key activities, resources, and partners determine what you need to operate and with whom you collaborate. Cost structure wraps it all up by detailing where money flows out.

Filling out the Business Model Canvas is like painting your business's portrait. Start by analysing each segment carefully, beginning with value propositions. Ask yourself: What problems do I solve for my customers? What needs do I fulfil? These questions guide the identification of benefits that set your business apart. Next, dive into customer segments. Who are they? What do they value? Tailor your offerings to their preferences. For channels, think about the best ways to reach them, whether through online platforms or physical stores. As for customer relationships, consider how you'll maintain connections; loyalty programs or personalised emails might be effective.

Key partners and resources are vital components. Identify alliances that bolster your operation, such as suppliers, distributors, and joint ventures. What resources do you need to deliver value? It could be technology, intellectual property, or skilled personnel. For revenue streams, explore diverse ways to generate income, including subscriptions, one-time sales, and possibly licensing fees. Lastly, review your cost structure by identifying fixed and variable costs involved in running your business.

To make this process engaging, imagine filling out the canvas as an exercise in creativity, akin to sketching on a blank canvas. Consider examples from different industries: Airbnb's canvas focuses on offering unique accommodations worldwide, while Uber emphasises convenient and affordable rides through their app. These examples illustrate how varied businesses utilise the canvas to define their strategies.

Once your canvas is complete, it's time to use it for strategy development. The Business Model Canvas isn't just a static document; it's a living tool that helps develop and test strategies. Use scenario planning to simulate different business situations and their impact on your model. What if a key partner pulls out? How would a new competitor entering the market impact your revenue streams? By playing out these scenarios, you prepare for potential challenges and opportunities.

Iteration is crucial; the business landscape shifts constantly, and so should your plans. Regularly revisit and update your canvas as your business evolves or as you gather new insights. Techniques for continuous refinement include seeking feedback from stakeholders, such as employees, customers, and advisors, and incorporating their perspectives into your model. Imagine it as tuning an instrument; slight adjustments can lead to harmony.

Feedback is invaluable; it offers fresh perspectives and uncovers blind spots in your strategy. Consider holding workshops with team members or stakeholders to review each segment of the canvas collectively. Encourage open discussions about what's working and where improvements can be made. This collaborative approach not only strengthens your model but also fosters a sense of ownership among participants.

Incorporating stakeholder feedback ensures that your business model remains relevant and responsive to changing market conditions or consumer preferences. If customers express interest in a new feature or service, integrating such feedback into your canvas allows you to pivot strategically rather than reactively.

As you build and iterate on your Business Model Canvas, remember that it's more than just an exercise in documentation; it's a dynamic tool that brings clarity and focus to your entrepreneurial endeavours. By understanding each component deeply and using the canvas strategically, you set yourself up for success in navigating the complexities of running a business.

THE THREE PILLARS OF BUSINESS:

Starting a business is an exciting journey filled with opportunities and challenges. As a first-time business owner, it's essential to understand the core disciplines that will drive your business towards success. Three key disciplines stand out among the myriad aspects of running a business: Sales, Finance, and Operations. These areas form the foundation upon which your business will grow and thrive.

Sales are the engine that generates revenue, ensuring that your business can sustain itself and expand. **Finance** provides the backbone, managing resources, planning for the future, and ensuring compliance with financial regulations. **Operations** is the heart of your business, encompassing the day-to-day activities that keep everything running smoothly and efficiently.

In this section, we will examine each of these disciplines and their interconnection to create a robust and successful business model. Additionally, more detailed chapters on each area are provided later. By mastering these areas, you will be well-equipped to navigate the complexities of entrepreneurship and build a strong foundation for your business.

KEY DISCIPLINES IN BUSINESS: SALES, FINANCE, AND OPERATIONS

Sales:

"People don't buy products; they buy solutions to their problems."

MARK TWAIN

Customers are the lifeblood of any business. To attract them, you need to generate sales. Without sales, there is no revenue, and a company cannot sustain itself. The sales discipline encompasses all activities related to selling products or services to customers. This includes:

- **Lead Generation**: Identifying potential customers who might be interested in your product or service.
- **Sales Strategy**: Developing a plan to reach, attract and persuade customers to make a purchase.
- **Customer Relationship Management (CRM)**: Building and maintaining relationships with customers to ensure repeat business and referrals.
- **Sales Techniques**: Utilising various methods, including direct sales, online sales, and retail sales, to close deals.
- **Performance Metrics**: Tracking sales performance through key metrics, including conversion rates, average deal size, and sales cycle length.

Effective sales strategies drive growth and help businesses reach their revenue targets.

Finance:

Finance is the backbone of a business, ensuring that all financial aspects are managed efficiently and effectively. This discipline involves:

- **Budgeting**: Planning how to allocate resources to various parts of the business.
- **Financial Planning and Analysis (FP&A)**: Forecasting future financial performance and analysing past performance to make informed decisions.
- **Accounting**: Keeping accurate records of all financial transactions, including income, expenses, assets, and liabilities.
- **Cash Flow Management**: Ensuring that the business has sufficient cash to meet its obligations, invest in growth opportunities, and pay you, allowing it to stay alive and continue operating.
- **Funding**: Securing capital through loans, investments, or other means to support business operations and expansion.
- **Compliance**: Adhering to financial regulations and standards to avoid legal issues and penalties.

A strong financial foundation enables a business to operate smoothly, make informed strategic investments, and weather economic fluctuations effectively.

Operations:

Operations involve the day-to-day activities that keep the business running. This discipline covers:

- **Production**: Manufacturing products or delivering services efficiently and to a high standard.
- **Supply Chain Management**: Managing the flow of

goods and services from suppliers to customers, ensuring timely delivery and quality control.

- **Process Optimisation**: Continuously improving business processes to increase efficiency and reduce costs.
- **Quality Assurance**: Ensuring that products or services meet the required standards and satisfy customer expectations.
- **Inventory Management**: Maintaining accurate stock levels to prevent shortages or excesses.
- **Logistics**: Coordinating the transportation and storage of goods.

Effective operations management ensures that the business can deliver its value proposition reliably and efficiently, leading to customer satisfaction and operational excellence.

FINANCIAL PROJECTIONS AND BUDGETING BASICS

Imagine embarking on an uncharted expedition without either a meticulously detailed map or a reliable GPS device to guide your journey. Financial projections can be vividly compared to that indispensable map, charting a course through the intricate financial terrain of your business's journey. This roadmap is not merely a series of numerical figures; it forms an essential segment of your comprehensive business plan, offering a strategic tool to forecast future financial outcomes. By delving into projected revenue streams, anticipated expenses, and potential cash flow dynamics, you gain a deeper understanding of your enterprise's prospective profitability and fiscal health. These forecasts serve as a navigational compass for strategic decision-making, underscoring to investors and lenders that your business concept possesses the promise of viability and enduring success.

There are three key financial planning tools to work on to check the viability of your business:

- Projected Profit & Loss Account
- Projected Cashflow
- Projected Balance Sheet

Whilst these are often in the realm of an accountant, you need to understand how much your business will cost before it starts making sales, and that you will have enough money to keep going before your customers pay you.

PROJECTED PROFIT & LOSS (P&L) STATEMENT

The P&L statement is a financial report that summarises the revenues, costs, and expenses incurred during a specific period. It shows how much profit or loss your business is making.

Projected Cash Flow Analysis

The cash flow analysis tracks the flow of cash in and out of your business, helping you understand your liquidity and ensuring you have sufficient money to cover expenses.

Crafting financial projections begins with the meticulous task of estimating revenue. Visualise this as akin to weather forecasting; you employ data analysis and market trends to predict future occurrences. Initiate this process by scrutinising the market size and gauging the potential demand for your product or service. Utilise historical data, if available, as a foundation, while incorporating emerging industry trends. A decisive aspect of this forecasting involves pricing strategy. Formulate a pricing approach that encapsulates the value proposition of your product while remaining attractive and competitive in the market.

Following the revenue estimates, developing an expense budget becomes essential. Think of expenses as the vital fuel that powers the engine of your business. Accurately accounting for all costs is crucial, distinguishing between fixed costs that remain constant and those variable costs that vary with production activity. Fixed costs, such as rental fees or employee salaries, stay the same, while variable expenses, like those related to raw materials and distribution, fluctuate with production levels. To compile a thorough budget, create a comprehensive list of all potential expenses and categorise them appropriately. Using a budget template at this stage can significantly enhance accuracy and efficiency, guiding you through various startup expenses, including equipment procurement, marketing initiatives, and legal compliance. Pay attention to often-overlooked startup costs, such as website development or the acquisition of office supplies, as these can accumulate rapidly, necessitating careful foresight and planning.

Cash flow management emerges as the vital energy of any business operation, encompassing the monetary movement in and out of your enterprise. It is crucial for sustaining daily functions and long-term viability. Healthy cash flow is essential; even the most financially sound businesses can struggle without it. Effective management involves careful monitoring of cash inflows and outflows, ensuring adequate liquidity to meet obligations as they arise. Utilising tools such as SAGE, QuickBooks, or Xero can significantly streamline this monitoring process by providing real-time insights into your financial status.

If this is not an area where you feel comfortable, the first person you should hire to assist you is a bookkeeper or an accountant. Many self-employed individuals are available, and a quick online search should help you find a suitable one, preferably with recommendations.

I insist that every enterprise I am involved in produces monthly management accounts and cashflow analysis, by which I can quickly determine its financial health.

Let's delve into a practical anecdote: the story of a small café owner facing cash flow challenges during the typically slow winter months. Through strategic initiatives such as offering gift cards in advance and launching appealing seasonal promotions, the café managed to maintain a steady cash flow, avoiding potential financial distress. This highlights the critical importance of proactive cash flow strategies in navigating seasonality.

Integrating these fundamental financial components into your business plan outlines your financial position and guides future actions. These financial projections go beyond simply persuading investors; they serve as a crucial tool for developing a thorough understanding of your business, enabling you to make informed and strategic decisions consistently.

These essential pillars are interconnected: vision, clear objectives, business models, and financial considerations. They all play a pivotal role in constructing the robust scaffolding of your venture. These elements provide clarity, direction, and a strong framework that paves the way for success. In our forthcoming chapter, we will explore the indispensable aspects of market research and how it underpins your strategy, ensuring that each progressive step is firmly rooted in knowledge and understanding.

CHAPTER 3
MASTERING MARKET RESEARCH

"Make what you can sell, not sell what you can make"

ALISTAIR CROLL

IDENTIFYING YOUR TARGET AUDIENCE

WHEN I FIRST VENTURED INTO business, I assumed everyone would love what I had to offer. I couldn't have been more wrong. Identifying your target audience is crucial; it is the backbone of a successful venture. It's like setting a stage where the audience is eager to hear your story. But who are they? Are they young professionals seeking innovation, or perhaps retirees looking for comfort? Understanding your audience can make or break your business. Let's break it down.

Demographics and psychographics form the crux of under-standing your audience. Demographics refer to the statistical characteristics of a population, such as age, gender, and income —basic yet essential markers that define who your audience might be. For example, if you are launching a line of high-end tech gadgets, it is vital to know that your target demographic consists of tech-savvy individuals aged 25 to 35 with disposable income.

On the other hand, psychographics delve deeper into your audience's minds, examining their lifestyle choices, values, and interests. Imagine knowing not just that your customers are professionals in their thirties, but that they value sustainability and enjoy outdoor activities. This level of understanding enables you to tailor your marketing messages in a way that resonates personally with them.

Creating detailed customer personas is next on your agenda. Picture this as painting vivid portraits of imaginary customers who embody your target market. These personas help you visualise your customers' needs and behaviours. Begin by gathering data through surveys and interviews, asking questions about their preferences and challenges. This information forms the foundation of your personas.

Next, compile this data into detailed profiles. Assign each persona a name and backstory to make them relatable. For example, meet "Eco-conscious Emma," a 29-year-old who prioritises sustainability in her purchases and loves hiking on weekends. Understanding Emma's world helps you shape products and messages that speak directly to her.

Persona Development Checklist

- Gather demographic data (age, gender, income).
- Collect psychographic insights (values, interests).
- Use surveys and interviews for detailed information.
- Create comprehensive profiles with names and backstories.

Social media is a goldmine for insights into audience behaviour. Platforms like Facebook Insights and 'X' Analytics offer a window into your audience's preferences and interactions. These tools reveal the content they engage with, the times they're most active, and their reactions to specific topics.

Social listening tools add another layer of depth, allowing you to monitor conversations about your brand or industry and provide real-time insights into customer sentiments. Imagine hearing first-hand what excites or frustrates potential customers; such information is invaluable for refining your approach.

Segmenting your audience elevates targeting to another level. It involves dividing your market into smaller segments based on specific criteria, such as geography or behaviour. This approach enables more personalised marketing efforts that address each segment's unique needs directly.

Investing time in this upfront will also lower your marketing costs and allow you to accurately identify your ideal customers without unnecessary waste.

Consider geographic segmentation if you're a local business looking to cater specifically to nearby customers. Behavioural segmentation focuses on customer actions, perhaps targeting those who frequently purchase online versus in-store shoppers.

Successful segmentation strategies abound; consider Netflix's ability to recommend shows based on user viewing habits, a prime example of behavioural segmentation. By analysing user data, Netflix tailors its offerings to individual preferences, enhancing user satisfaction.

Incorporating these strategies into your business arsenal ensures you are not merely speaking to an audience but engaging with them on a meaningful level. Understanding who they are and what they value transforms potential customers into loyal advocates for your brand.

ANALYSING COMPETITORS EFFECTIVELY

Understanding your competitors, much like taking on the role of a diligent detective in the intricate world of business, demands a sharp eye for detail and a strategic mindset. It involves a comprehensive examination of what other entities in your sector are doing, dissecting their strategies, deciphering what they excel at, and critically analysing where they may be faltering.

Any insights you uncover are invaluable and can guide your business strategy. The first step in this intricate process involves identifying your main competitors. Interestingly, they may not always be the ones you initially perceive; often, they exist within the same industry, yet at other times, they may offer products or services that are different but cater to the same market audience.

Once you have curated this list, produce a SWOT analysis. This analytical tool is paramount in pinpointing their strengths, weaknesses, opportunities, and potential threats. For instance, a competitive adversary might possess a robust brand image yet simultaneously suffer from poor customer service, an area ripe for exploitation.

UNVEILING HIDDEN VULNERABILITIES

Identifying these weaknesses resembles finding a crucial, missing piece of an intricate puzzle. This recognition allows you to intervene and offer a superior alternative. Your competitive advantage stems from discerning the unique value you can provide or execute differently and more swiftly. It might be rooted in expediting delivery services, offering more person-alised customer engagement, or presenting a niche product that others in the industry have yet to consider. Reflect on companies like Netflix, which initially recognised and filled a significant gap that traditional video rental stores left through their innovative streaming service. They identified an unmet consumer need and capitalised on it with exceptional success.

When we launched a high-level Executive Search division in our business, we were a small fish in a big pond surrounded by established names. What we quickly learned, however, was that these firms sent senior partners to pitch for work, while junior employees conducted the assignments, which meant clients soon noticed a disconnect between what they purchased and what they received. To compete in this environment, we assured clients that the person they met to sell our services would be the one carrying out the work and their main point of contact throughout the project, thereby creating a competitive advantage over larger, more established brands.

This, however, is just the initial phase of gathering intelligence. Once you are equipped with this intel, progress towards benchmarking, which involves comparing your business against these competitors to evaluate how you measure up. The essence of benchmarking lies in establishing performance standards that align with your industry's key performance indicators (KPIs), thus serving as a metric for how your business performs in crucial areas compared to other market players. Important KPIs may include customer satisfaction scores, delivery timelines, or cost efficiency metrics. Remember, this endeavour isn't mere imitation; it's about understanding areas where you can improve and recognising where you already excel.

STRATEGIC INTEGRATION

Integrating this competitor insight into your strategic planning processes is imperative. Use the acquired knowledge to sculpt and refine your business strategies moving forward. Perhaps this means augmenting your product features in response to customer demands unmet elsewhere, or maybe it's about enhancing your marketing message to accentuate your distinctive benefits.

Consider the approach of renowned brands like Apple, which wield competitive insights in their relentless pursuit of staying ahead of the curve. Apple doesn't just follow prevailing trends, they redefine them by astutely analysing competitors' moves and consistently going the extra mile. For instance, when the market was saturated with keyboard-centric phones, Apple unveiled the iPhone with its revolutionary touchscreen technology, fundamentally altering the technological landscape.

ANTICIPATING MARKET SHIFTS

As you make your next strategic moves, please keep in mind that this analysis is a dynamic, ongoing process. Markets are in a state of perpetual evolution, new competitors ceaselessly emerge, and consumer preferences are in constant flux. By vigilantly monitoring competitors regularly, you ensure that your strategies maintain relevance and efficacy.

This methodology of strategic thinking has the potential to be truly transformative for your business. It unearths possibilities you might not have previously contemplated, thereby propelling you towards continuous innovation and improvement. In the rapidly evolving world of entrepreneurship, those who adeptly adapt and proactively learn from their surroundings are the entities that ultimately thrive.

Therefore, embrace that detective hat and wear it with pride as you venture into the complex dynamics of competition surrounding you. Let these insights steer every decision, from product development to crafting marketing strategies, ensuring that your business excels by deliberate design.

LEVERAGING DATA COLLECTION TECHNIQUES

In this fast-paced world, understanding your market is more crucial than ever. Whether you're launching a new product or refining an existing service, the foundation often lies in robust data collection. Let's start with the basics: primary and secondary research. Primary research is akin to gathering first-hand insights directly from the source. Think of it like having a heart-to-heart with your customers. Surveys and focus groups fall into this category, allowing you to dig deeper into your audience's thoughts and feelings. On the other hand, secondary research involves the analysis of existing data, like reading a well-researched paper that captures broader market trends. Industry reports and academic studies can provide valuable context, helping you see where your business fits within the larger picture.

When it comes to designing effective surveys, tools like Survey-Monkey and Google Forms are your best friends. These platforms offer user-friendly interfaces that make survey creation a breeze. But remember, a survey is only as good as its questions. Aim for clarity and precision, avoiding leading questions that could skew results. Think about asking open-ended questions for qualitative insights, alongside multiple-choice options for quantitative data. Distributing these surveys strategically can yield a wealth of information, painting a clearer picture of your market's desires and needs.

Focus groups hold a special place in consumer research. They provide a unique opportunity to observe group dynamics and uncover insights that might not surface in one-on-one interactions. Imagine sitting in a room where your potential customers discuss their likes and dislikes about your product. It's an eye-opening experience that can reveal nuances you never considered. Organising a focus group requires careful planning. Start by selecting participants who represent your target audience. Create an environment where participants feel comfortable sharing their thoughts openly. As a moderator, guide the discussion without dominating it, allowing organic conversations to unfold. This approach often uncovers rich insights that surveys alone might miss.

Once you've gathered data through surveys and focus groups, the real work begins, analysing and interpreting it to extract meaningful insights. Data analysis tools and prompting an AI platform can make this task more manageable, helping you identify patterns and trends within the data.

VISUALISING DATA WITH CHARTS AND GRAPHS

Visual representations of data provide clarity amidst complexity. Consider creating bar charts to compare customer preferences or pie charts to illustrate market share distribution. Line graphs can show trends over time, revealing customer behaviour patterns or seasonal fluctuations in demand.

As you sift through the data, remember that it's not just about numbers; it's about stories. Each data point represents a voice, an opinion, or a preference that can shape your business decisions. Look for correlations between different variables. Does an increase in social media engagement correlate with higher sales? Are there common themes among dissatisfied customers? These connections can guide strategic shifts and innovations.

Data interpretation isn't just a one-off job; it's an ongoing process that informs your business strategy at every stage. As markets evolve, so do consumer preferences and behaviours. Regularly revisiting your data collection efforts ensures you remain attuned to shifting trends and emerging opportunities.

Incorporating these techniques into your business strategy gives you the knowledge to make informed decisions rooted in real-world insights, whether refining products based on customer feedback or identifying new market segments ripe for exploration. Working with comprehensive data collection techniques leads you toward meaningful growth.

As we explore further aspects of market research throughout this chapter, keep these foundational principles in mind; they serve as the bedrock upon which successful businesses build their strategies and navigate the ever-changing landscape of entrepreneurship.

TRANSLATING MARKET RESEARCH INTO BUSINESS STRATEGY

Market research isn't just a box to tick. It's the foundation of strategic planning. But how do you transform raw data into actionable strategies? The answer lies in connecting insights to strategy. You must sift through the findings and identify patterns that inform your next move. Imagine a map where the data points guide you toward opportunities and away from potential pitfalls. For instance, a small café might discover through research that its customers crave more plant-based options. Armed with this insight, the café can strategically pivot its menu, attracting a broader customer base and enhancing customer satisfaction.

Prioritising insights is equally crucial. Not every piece of data is actionable. You must decide what is worth your time and resources. Decision matrices can be helpful here, allowing you to weigh the impact and feasibility of potential actions. Picture this: laid out before you are several research findings, each clamouring for attention. Some may promise substantial rewards but require significant investment, while others offer smaller benefits with minimal effort. A decision matrix helps you rank these opportunities, streamlining your focus towards initiatives that promise the greatest return.

Once you've prioritised your insights, the next step is implementing research-driven changes. This is where strategy becomes tangible. For example, consider a retail store that identifies a demand for eco-friendly products through customer feedback. It might decide to switch suppliers, opting for sustainable materials. This change aligns with customer values and positions the store as a forward-thinking brand in a competitive market. Successful implementation strategies often include pilot programs or phased rollouts, allowing for adjustments based on real-world feedback.

Consistent monitoring and adaptation are key to sustaining strategic success. The business landscape is ever-changing, and strategies must evolve accordingly. Regular strategy reviews ensure your approach remains relevant and effective. Set aside time each quarter to evaluate your progress, examining both successes and areas for improvement. Feedback loops play a vital role here, providing insights into what's working and what needs tweaking. These loops can involve direct customer feedback, employee input, or market trend analysis.

Imagine your business as a ship navigating through uncharted waters. Market research serves as your compass, offering direction amid uncertainty. But without ongoing monitoring and adaptation, even the best-laid plans can go awry. Techniques like quarterly strategy reviews help keep your course steady. They allow you to assess whether you're meeting your goals or if adjustments are necessary. By staying attuned to changes in consumer behaviour or industry trends, you ensure your strategies remain agile and responsive.

Feedback loops further enhance this adaptability by offering real-time insights into the effectiveness of your strategies. You can encourage open communication with customers and employees alike; their perspectives often show hidden opportunities or challenges you might not have considered. For instance, an online retailer might launch a new feature based on customer suggestions and monitor its impact through sales data and user reviews.

Incorporating these elements into your strategic planning process cultivates a culture of continuous improvement within your organisation. It fosters an environment where learning from successes and failures becomes second nature, a mindset propelling businesses toward sustainable growth.

Remember that data is not merely numbers on a page; it's a story waiting to be told, a story of consumer needs, market dynamics, and business potential. By effectively connecting insights to strategy, prioritising impactful actions, implementing changes thoughtfully, and embracing continuous monitoring, you transform market research from a static exercise into an ongoing dialogue that shapes your business's future.

CHAPTER 4
NAVIGATING LEGAL AND REGULATORY LANDSCAPES

REGISTERING YOUR BUSINESS NAME AND ENTITY

BEFORE YOU EMBARK on your business voyage, you need a sturdy vessel, your business's legal structure. Choosing the proper business structure can feel like picking the right ship for your journey. Each type of entity, from sole proprietorships, partnerships, to Limited Liability Companies (LLC), (also known as Private Limited Companies in the UK), and Publicly Listed Companies (PLCs), offers different benefits and challenges.

Depending on your country, this process will slightly differ, but in most cases will follow a similar procedure. For this book, we will look at the UK and the USA.

Sole proprietorships are straightforward, giving you complete control but leaving your personal assets exposed; there is no distinction between your business and your personal assets, rendering them vulnerable if your creditors (people you owe money to), seek repayment, should your business become insolvent and unable to pay them.

Private Limited Companies/LLCs, on the other hand, blend simplicity with liability protection, shielding your personal finances from business debts. Public Listed Companies (PLC's) stand as the super tankers of the business world, offering robust protection but demanding more rigorous compliance and tax obligations.

Understanding tax implications is equally vital:

Sole proprietors face personal income tax on profits, whilst Ltd's/LLCs offer additional flexibility, with company profits taxed first as Corporation Tax, a provision for which is ideally made as profits grow and cash is received. Secondly, when you withdraw money from your business, either as Pay As You Earn (PAYE) or as dividends,

With a company, you are in effect dealing with double taxation, both at a corporate and personal level. However, they also provide avenues for tax deductions that other entities may not offer.

It is essential that you understand what business expenses are and what are not allowed for tax relief. For example, in the UK you may pay for legitimate client entertainment and hospitality through your business. However, the amount spent will still incur corporation tax, as it is not tax-deductible. So, you'll need to make a financial provision for this amount of tax in your cash flow planning.

You must also know when your tax is due and prepare for it accordingly.

Filing the necessary paperwork is your next port of call.

HOW TO REGISTER A COMPANY IN THE UK: A STEP-BY-STEP GUIDE

Setting up a company in the UK follows a structured process that involves several key steps to ensure legal compliance and operational readiness. Firstly, you need to choose a unique company name that is not too similar to existing businesses, which can be verified on the Companies House website. Next, decide on the business structure that best suits your needs, such as a Private Limited Company (Ltd), sole trader, partnership, or public limited company (PLC). Appoint at least one director to manage the company and consider whether you require a company secretary for administrative support. Prepare the necessary documents, including the Memorandum of Association and Articles of Association, which outline the company's rules and agreements. Register your company with Companies House, either online or by post, and select a Standard Industrial Classification (SIC) code that reflects your business activities. Once registered, you must also register for Corporation Tax within three months and consider other tax registrations like VAT and PAYE. Open a business bank account to keep your finances separate from personal funds, and secure any required licences and permits based on your industry and location. Maintaining compliance with annual reports, tax obligations, and accurate record-keeping is essential for the ongoing success of your business. By following these steps, you can ensure that your company is legally established and ready to operate in the UK.

Consider appointing an Accountant to help you with this process and the ongoing statutory reporting of your business, which will enable you to focus on what you do best.

Here's a checklist to help you through the process:

Choose a Company Name

- **Unique Name**: Ensure your company name is unique and not too similar to existing companies.
- **Restrictions**: Avoid sensitive words or expressions unless you have permission to use them.

Select a Business Structure

- **Private Limited Company (Ltd)**: The most common structure, where the company is a separate legal entity from its owners.
- **Other Structures**: Consider other structures like sole trader, partnership, or public limited company (PLC) based on your business needs.

Choose Directors and a Company Secretary

- **Directors**: You must appoint at least one director responsible for running the company.
- **Company Secretary**: Optional for private limited companies, but can be useful for administrative tasks.

Decide Who the Shareholders or Guarantors Are

- **Shareholders**: Must have at least one shareholder. Shareholders own the company and have voting rights.
- **Guarantors**: For companies limited by guarantee, guarantors agree to contribute a certain amount if the company is wound up.

Prepare Your Documents

- **Memorandum of Association**: A legal statement signed by all initial shareholders or guarantors agreeing to form the company.
- **Articles of Association:** These are the written rules that govern the company's operations and are agreed upon by the shareholders or guarantors, directors, and the company secretary.

Register with Companies House

- **Online Registration**: You can register online through the Companies House website; the process usually takes 24 hours.
- **Postal Registration**: Alternatively, you can register by post using form IN01. This takes 8 to 10 days.
- **SIC Code**: Choose a Standard Industrial Classification (SIC) code that describes your business activities.

Register for Taxes

- **Corporation Tax**: Register for Corporation Tax within three months of starting to do business.
- **Other Taxes**: Depending on your business, you may need to register for VAT, PAYE for employers, and other taxes.

Open a Business Bank Account

- **Separate Account**: It's important to keep your business finances separate from your personal finances.
- **Documents Needed**: You'll need your certificate of incorporation, proof of identity, and proof of address.

Additional Steps

- **Set Up Accounting Records**: Keep accurate financial records and prepare for annual accounts and tax returns.
- **Comply with Legal Requirements**: Ensure you comply with ongoing legal requirements, such as filing annual confirmation statements and maintaining statutory registers.

HOW TO REGISTER A COMPANY IN THE USA: A STEP-BY-STEP GUIDE

For an LLC or corporation, this involves submitting articles of incorporation or organisation to your state's Secretary of State office. These documents establish the foundation for your entity's legal existence, detailing key information such as your business name, address, and management structure. If you plan to operate under a name different from your registered one, a DBA (Doing Business As) filing is necessary. This step ensures transparency and legal compliance, informing consumers about who they're truly dealing with.

A registered agent plays a crucial role in maintaining your business's legal standing. Consider them as your trusted liaison for all legal matters. They manage critical documents such as tax forms and legal notices on your behalf. When choosing a registered agent, consider their reliability and accessibility—this role is vital in ensuring you don't miss important notifications that could affect your business operations. Many businesses opt for professional registered agent services to guarantee continuity, particularly if they operate across multiple states.

Registering a company in the USA involves several steps and requires specific documentation. Here's a comprehensive guide to help you through the process:

Choose a Business Structure

- **Sole Proprietorship**: Simple to set up, but the owner assumes full liability.
- **Partnership**: Suitable for businesses with two or more owners; liability is shared.
- **Limited Liability Company (LLC)**: Offers liability protection and tax flexibility.
- **Corporation**: A more complex structure, ideal for

companies seeking investors or a public listing. This includes S-Corps and C-Corps.

Select a State for Registration

- **Business-Friendly States:** States such as Delaware, Nevada, and Wyoming are frequently favoured by entrepreneurs because of their pro-business environments, advantageous tax structures, and streamlined administrative requirements.
- **Considerations:** Each state has distinct business regulations, tax structures, and compliance requirements. Select a state that corresponds with your business needs.

Choose and Register Your Business Name

- **Unique Name:** Ensure your business name is unique and not too similar to existing companies. Conduct a name search in the chosen state's business registry.
- **DBA (Doing Business As):** If you plan to operate under a name other than your own, you may need to file a DBA.

File Registration Documents with the State

- **Articles of Incorporation/Organisation:** Prepare and file the necessary documents with the state's Secretary of State office. This includes the Articles of Incorporation for corporations or the Articles of Organisation for LLCs.
- **Filing Fees:** Pay the required filing fees, which vary by state.

Obtain an EIN (Employer Identification Number)

- **IRS Registration**: Apply for an EIN from the Internal Revenue Service (IRS). This number is used for tax purposes and is required for opening a business bank account and hiring employees.
- **Online Application**: You can apply for an EIN online through the IRS website.

Open a Business Bank Account

- **Separate Account**: It's important to keep your business finances separate from your personal finances.
- **Documents Needed**: You'll need your EIN, Articles of Incorporation/Organisation, and proof of identity.

Secure Business Licenses and Permits

- **Federal, State, and Local Licenses**: Depending on your business type and location, you may be required to obtain various licenses and permits. Check with federal, state, and local authorities to ensure compliance.
- **Industry-Specific Requirements:** Certain industries, including healthcare, food services, and construction, have particular licensing requirements.

Maintain Compliance

- **Annual Reports**: Many states require businesses to file annual reports and pay annual fees.
- **Taxes**: Ensure compliance with federal, state, and local tax obligations, including income tax, sales tax, and employment taxes.
- **Record Keeping**: Maintain accurate financial records and minutes of meetings (for corporations).

ADDITIONAL TIPS FOR ENTREPRENEURS

Legal and Tax Advice: Consider consulting a business lawyer and a tax advisor to navigate the complexities of business regulations and tax laws, regardless of where you are registering your business.

For an LLC or corporation, this entails submitting articles of incorporation or organisation to your state's Secretary of State office. These documents establish the foundation for your entity's legal existence, outlining essential information such as your business name, address, and management structure. If you plan to operate under a name different from your registered one, a DBA (Doing Business As) filing is necessary. This step promotes transparency and legal compliance, informing consumers who they are truly dealing with.

A registered agent plays a pivotal role in maintaining your business's legal standing. Consider them a trusted liaison for all legal matters. They handle critical documents such as tax forms and legal notices on your behalf. When choosing a registered agent, prioritise reliability and accessibility; their role is essential in ensuring that you do not miss vital notifications which could impact your business operations. Many businesses opt for professional registered agent services to guarantee continuity, particularly if they operate across states.

Registering Your Business Checklist:

- **Step 1**: Identify the business structure that best suits your needs.
- **Step 2**: Conduct a thorough name availability search using state registries and trademark databases.
- **Step 3**: File the necessary paperwork with the appropriate government offices.
- **Step 4**: Choose a reliable registered agent to handle legal documents.

Completing these steps lays the foundation for your venture, ensuring you navigate the initial stages of establishing your business smoothly. By understanding and navigating these legal requirements meticulously, you're not just protecting yourself—you're fortifying your business's future.

UNDERSTANDING TAX OBLIGATIONS AND BENEFITS

When you start a business, understanding taxes can feel like navigating a vast, intricate maze. Taxes are an inevitable part of running a business, appearing in various forms, including corporation tax, income tax, sales tax or VAT, and self-employment tax.

Once more, I have divided the following section into UK and USA taxation to offer you precise guidance:

Types of Taxation for UK Businesses and Business Owners

Understanding the various types of taxation in the UK is essential for business owners to ensure compliance and effective financial planning. Below is an overview of the main taxes that UK businesses and business owners should be aware of:

Corporation Tax

Corporation tax is imposed on the profits of limited companies, foreign companies operating with a UK branch or office, and other unincorporated associations such as clubs and cooperatives. As of 2025, the standard corporation tax rate is 25% for companies with profits exceeding £250,000. Companies with profits of £50,000 or less qualify for a small profits rate of 19%.

This tax pertains to profits derived from business activities, investments, and asset sales.

These taxes are paid annually unless profits exceed £1.5 million per annum, in which case they are due quarterly. Please note that profit refers to the amount your accounts indicate you have invoiced after costs; this may not be the cash currently in your bank account, but rather money that is still owed to you.

Dividend Tax

Shareholders who receive dividends from their investments in a company must pay dividend tax. The rates for dividend tax are lower than income tax rates but apply to dividend income that exceeds the dividend allowance.

Income Tax

Sole traders and partners in a business partnership are responsible for paying income tax on their earnings. The income tax rates are progressive, ranging from 20% to 45%, depending on the income bracket.

For the tax year 2025-2026, the personal allowance (the amount of income that can be earned before paying income tax) is £12,570. Income tax also applies to rental income, income from trusts, pensions, and interest on savings.

Value Added Tax (VAT)

VAT is a consumption tax levied on most goods and services supplied by VAT-registered businesses. The standard VAT rate is 20%, with reduced rates of 5% applicable to certain goods and services, and a zero rate for others.

Businesses must register for VAT if their annual turnover exceeds £90,000. VAT-registered businesses can reclaim the VAT they incur on business-related purchases.

National Insurance Contributions (NICs)

National Insurance is paid by employees, employers, and self-employed individuals. It funds state benefits such as the NHS and the state pension. Employers pay NICs on their employees' earnings above a certain threshold, while employees have NICs deducted from their wages. Self-employed individuals pay Class 2 and Class 4 NICs based on their profits. From April 2025, you will pay 15% Employers' NIC on all wages; this is in addition to the personal NIC paid by the employee.

Pay As You Earn (PAYE)

PAYE is a system for collecting income tax and National Insurance contributions (NICs) from employees' wages. Employers are responsible for deducting these amounts from their employees' pay and remitting them to HM Revenue and Customs (HMRC). This system ensures that employees' tax liabilities are settled throughout the year.

Dividend Tax

Shareholders who receive dividends from their investments in a company must pay dividend tax. The rates for dividend tax are lower than those for income tax, but they apply to dividend income exceeding the dividend allowance. As of 2025, the dividend allowance is £2,000.

Business Rates

Business rates tax non-domestic properties, including shops, offices, and factories. The amount payable is determined by the property's rateable value, as assessed by the Valuation Office Agency. Businesses operating from home may also be liable for business rates if a substantial part of the property is utilised for business purposes.

Additional local authority charges may also apply to your business for staff car parking and waste removal.

TYPES OF TAXATION FOR US BUSINESSES AND BUSINESS OWNERS

Understanding the various types of taxation in the United States is essential for business owners to ensure compliance and effective financial planning. Here's an overview of the main taxes that businesses and business owners in the USA need to be aware of:

Income Tax

All businesses must submit annual income tax returns, except for partnerships, which submit annual information returns.

The form you use depends on your business structure:

- **Corporations (C Corps)**: Subject to a flat corporate tax rate of 21%
- **Sole Proprietorships, Partnerships, LLCs, and S Corporations**: These entities are typically pass-through entities, meaning the income is reported on the owners' personal tax returns and taxed at individual income tax rates ranging from 10% to 37%.

Self-Employment Tax

Self-employment tax is a social security and Medicare tax primarily for individuals who work for themselves. It is similar to the social security and Medicare taxes withheld from employees' wages by their employers. Self-employed individuals must file Schedule SE with their federal income tax return and pay self-employment tax if their net earnings from self-employment are $400 or more.

Employment Taxes

When you have employees, you are responsible for several employment taxes, including:

- **Social Security and Medicare Taxes**: Employers must withhold these taxes from employees' wages and pay a matching amount.
- **Federal Income Tax Withholding**: Employers must withhold federal income tax from employees' wages.
- **Federal Unemployment Tax (FUTA)**: Employers pay FUTA tax to provide unemployment benefits to workers who have lost their jobs.

Excise Tax

Excise duties are levied on specific goods, services, and activities. Businesses may be liable for excise duty if they manufacture or sell certain products, operate specific types of businesses, utilise various kinds of equipment, facilities, or products, or receive payment for particular services. The duty may be imposed on the manufacturer, retailer, or consumer, depending on the specific tax.

Estimated Tax

Businesses and individuals must pay taxes as they earn or receive income during the year, either through withholding or estimated tax payments. Estimated taxes are used to pay income tax and other taxes, such as self-employment tax. Individuals, including sole proprietors, partners, and S corporation shareholders, generally must make estimated tax payments if they expect to owe at least $1,000 in tax after subtracting withholding and tax credits.

Sales Tax

Sales tax is a state-level tax imposed on the sale of goods and services. The rate and rules vary by state. Businesses are responsible for collecting sales tax from customers at the point of sale and remitting it to the state tax authority.

Property Tax

Property tax is imposed on real estate and sometimes on personal property owned by a business. The rate and rules vary by locality. Businesses must pay property tax based on the assessed value of their property.

Wherever your business is based, it is essential that you also understand the tax calendar for filing accounts and paying your tax bill. This is where seeking the advice of a professional accountant or CPA in the USA is essential to help you plan and free your time to get on with growing your business.

PROTECTING INTELLECTUAL PROPERTY

In the vast landscape of business, safeguarding your intellectual property (IP) is akin to securing the crown jewels of your enterprise. IP encompasses the creations of the mind, including inventions, literary works, designs, symbols, and even confidential business information. Understanding the various types of IP protection is essential as you build your business. Patents, for instance, grant inventors exclusive rights to their inventions for a specific period, preventing others from making, using, or selling the invention without permission. This is particularly vital for businesses that flourish on innovation and new product development. Copyrights protect original works of authorship, such as books, music, and art. They ensure that creators hold exclusive rights to use and distribute their creations. While patents focus on functional inventions, copyrights safeguard creative expressions.

Trademarks, on the other hand, safeguard brand identities. They protect any word, phrase, symbol, or design that distinguishes your goods or services from others. Think of iconic brands like Nike's swoosh or McDonald's golden arches; these are powerful trademarks that instantly evoke brand recognition and trust. Trade secrets are another form of IP protection, covering confidential business information that provides you with a competitive edge. This could be anything from a secret formula to proprietary manufacturing processes.

Securing these rights involves a structured process. Filing for trademarks and patents requires diligence and precision. For trademarks, start by conducting a thorough search to ensure your mark isn't already in use. Once you're certain your trademark is unique, submit an application that includes a detailed description of the mark and its intended use. The patent process is more intricate. Begin by ensuring your invention is novel and non-obvious. You'll need to prepare detailed drawings and descriptions that illustrate how your invention works. The application process can be lengthy and complex, often necessitating the assistance of a patent attorney.

Once you have secured your IP rights, it is essential to maintain and enforce them to prevent infringement. Regularly monitor the market for unauthorised use of your trademarks or patents. This vigilance may involve setting up Google Alerts or using specialised monitoring services to track potential infringements. If you spot a violation, legal actions are available to protect your rights. Sending a cease-and-desist letter is often the first step, signalling your intent to enforce your IP rights. For more serious infringements, you may need to pursue litigation or seek mediation.

Licensing your intellectual property presents another opportunity for generating revenue. By permitting others to utilise your IP under specific terms, you can create an additional income stream while retaining ownership. Licensing agreements are essential in this process, as they delineate how your IP may be employed and what compensation you will receive in return. For instance, a software company might license its code to other developers, thereby expanding its reach while generating royalties.

The benefits of IP licensing for startups are significant. It allows companies to scale without the need for extensive capital investment. By leveraging existing intellectual assets, startups can focus on growth and innovation while partners bring products to new markets. Licensing also fosters collaboration and opens doors to new opportunities and networks.

As you navigate the world of intellectual property protection, remember that it's not just about securing your ideas; it's about strategically positioning your business for long-term success in a competitive market. Your IP is a valuable asset that deserves vigilant protection and smart utilisation.

NAVIGATING LICENSES, PERMITS, AND REGULATIONS

Stepping into the realm of entrepreneurship requires more than just a brilliant idea and a robust business plan. You must ensure that your venture complies with various legal obligations, beginning with obtaining the necessary licences and permits. The challenge here is that the requirements can vary significantly depending on your industry and location. For instance, if you're opening a restaurant, you'll need health permits and food handler certifications. Conversely, a home-based consulting business might require fewer permits but still needs to adhere to other regulations. Understanding these specifics is crucial. Start by visiting local government websites or business resource centres to identify what applies to your particular business type. These resources often provide comprehensive lists of industry-specific licensing requirements, ensuring you don't overlook any critical steps.

Once you've identified the licences and permits you need, it's time to tackle the application process. Many government organisations offer online portals that simplify this task, allowing you to complete forms and submit payments digitally. This convenience saves time and effort, especially as you manage various start-up tasks. However, it's important to budget for these permits, as costs can vary widely depending on your location and industry. Research these costs early on to include them in your initial budget, avoiding any unwelcome surprises.

Understanding and adhering to industry regulations is another critical aspect of running a successful business. These regulations are established to ensure safety, fairness, and quality across various sectors. For instance, if you're launching a food-related business, you'll need to comply with the standards set by regulatory bodies. These may include guidelines for food safety, labelling, and packaging, all designed to protect consumers. Developing compliance checklists specific to your industry can be invaluable in this context. Such checklists serve as practical tools to help you track essential requirements and ensure you're consistently meeting them.

Staying updated on regulatory changes is vital for maintaining compliance over time. Regulations can evolve as new laws are enacted, so it's important to keep your finger on the pulse of any changes that might affect your business. Subscribing to industry newsletters is one way to stay informed about updates in your field. These newsletters often provide insights into upcoming regulatory changes, allowing you to prepare in advance. Participating in workshops and seminars is another excellent strategy. These events offer opportunities to learn from experts, ask questions, and network with other business owners facing similar challenges.

Compliance Checklist: Licenses and Permits

- Identify industry-specific licenses required for your business.
- Research permits for physical locations.
- Apply for licenses through online government portals.
- Budget for permit costs based on industry and location.
- Develop compliance checklists tailored to your sector's regulations.

In summary, navigating the world of licenses, permits, and regulations is a fundamental step in establishing a legally compliant business. By understanding the specific requirements for your industry, applying for necessary licenses efficiently, adhering to regulations, and staying updated on changes, you lay the groundwork for success. This foundation not only protects you legally but also builds trust with customers who appreciate your commitment to quality and safety.

CHAPTER 5
EXPLORING FINANCING OPTIONS

BOOTSTRAPPING: STARTING LEAN AND MEAN

IF YOU THINK the idea of securing funding for your business is daunting, enter bootstrapping, a strategy that empowers you to build your business using your own resources and ingenuity. In the entrepreneurial world, bootstrapping means utilising personal finances, operating revenues, and creative problem-solving to fuel your venture's growth without external investors. This approach allows you to maintain full ownership and control, ensuring your vision remains at the forefront without compromise.

Bootstrapping offers several advantages beyond mere financial independence. By keeping control within your grasp, you can steer your company in the direction you envision without external interference. This autonomy is invaluable, especially when your business is in its early stages. Moreover, the discipline required in managing limited resources can sharpen decision-making skills, fostering a mindset of frugality and innovation. Entrepreneurs who bootstrap often cultivate resilience, finding innovative ways to stretch every penny. The constraints of limited funding can inspire creativity, prompting you to explore unconventional solutions to challenges.

When bootstrapping, prioritising essential expenses is paramount. It's crucial to distinguish between must-haves and nice-to-haves, directing funds towards activities that directly contribute to building your product or service. Consider starting small and scaling gradually as your resources allow. Embrace the philosophy of lean startup methodology; launching with a minimum viable product (MVP) enables you to test concepts without overcommitting financially. Utilise personal savings, lines of credit, and assets where possible. If you've set aside a rainy-day fund, now might be the time to tap into it strategically.

Practical strategies abound for stretching limited resources further. Bartering services with other entrepreneurs can be mutually beneficial, exchanging skills or products without monetary transactions. Instead of renting office space right away, consider working from home or utilising coworking spaces that offer flexible terms. Automating repetitive tasks with free or low-cost software can save both time and money, streamlining operations while reducing employment costs.

Success stories of bootstrapped businesses provide inspiration and proof that it's possible to thrive without external funding. Take Mailchimp, for example. The founders built their email marketing platform from scratch while maintaining complete ownership. Today, Mailchimp serves millions of users worldwide. Another example is Spanx, founded by Sara Blakely with just $5,000 in savings. Her innovative shapewear revolutionised the industry, demonstrating how determination and resourcefulness can lead to extraordinary success.

As your business grows, managing expansion with limited resources requires strategic planning. Maximising cash flow becomes critical, monitor income closely and delay unnecessary expenses until revenue stabilises. Focus on high-impact marketing strategies that offer maximum reach for minimal cost.

Social media platforms provide an excellent opportunity to engage potential customers without breaking the bank.

Creative cost-saving measures are essential for staying afloat during lean times. Negotiate favourable terms with suppliers by highlighting potential long-term partnerships. Explore bulk purchasing options when feasible; volume discounts can significantly reduce per-unit costs. Additionally, consider outsourcing non-core functions, such as bookkeeping or graphic design, to freelancers rather than hiring full-time staff.

Maintaining a lean budget doesn't mean sacrificing growth; it means being strategic in how you allocate resources. By focusing on efficiency and leveraging existing assets creatively, you position your business for sustainable success even in resource-constrained environments.

Bootstrapping Success Reflection

Reflect on the approaches outlined here: What strategies resonate most with your entrepreneurial vision? How can you apply these principles to effectively navigate financial challenges? Consider journalling about your current financial priorities and identifying areas where you might implement cost-saving measures or utilise personal assets more efficiently.

When exploring bootstrapping as a viable financing option, remember that the journey demands dedication and adaptability, while also offering unparalleled rewards in terms of control over your venture's destiny. Bootstrapping is not merely about making do with less; it involves cultivating resilience and innovation, a mindset that will serve well throughout your entrepreneurial endeavours.

SEEKING FUNDING FROM FAMILY AND FRIENDS

It's likely that you have shared some ideas for your exciting venture with family and friends; depending on their circumstances, they can be one of the most accessible sources of initial funding. While this approach has its advantages, it also presents unique challenges and considerations. Here's a guide to help you navigate this process effectively.

Advantages of Seeking Funding from Family and Friends

Accessibility: Family and friends are often more approachable than traditional investors or banks. They may be inclined to support your business idea due to their personal relationship with you.

Flexible Terms: Unlike formal investors, family and friends may provide more accommodating repayment terms and lower interest rates, or even offer funds as a gift or grant.

Trust and Support: These individuals are likely to have faith in you and your vision, offering not only financial backing but also moral encouragement.

Preparing for the Ask

Before seeking funding from family and friends, it is essential to prepare thoroughly. Here are some steps to ensure you present your request professionally:

Develop a Business Plan: Create a detailed business plan that outlines your business idea, target market, revenue model, and financial projections. This shows that you are serious and have thought through your venture.

Determine Funding Needs: Clearly outline the amount of money required and its intended use. Detail the costs and describe how the funds will contribute to your business's success.

Consider the Terms: Determine whether you are seeking a loan, investment, or gift. If it's a loan, outline the repayment terms. If it's an investment, explain the potential returns and risks.

Making the Pitch

When you're ready to ask for funding, approach the conversation with professionalism and respect. Here are some tips for making your pitch:

Be Honest and Transparent: Clearly communicate the risks involved and the potential for loss. Honesty fosters trust and demonstrates respect for their contribution.

Show Commitment: Demonstrate your commitment to the business by sharing the steps your previous experiences and your aspirations for the future.

Provide Documentation: Supply copies of your business plan, financial projections, and any other pertinent documents. This aids them in understanding your business and making an informed decision.

Managing Relationships

Seeking financial support from family and friends can affect your personal relationships. Here's how to manage these dynamics:

Set Clear Expectations: Ensure that everyone comprehends the terms of the funding and the potential outcomes. Clear communication helps to prevent misunderstandings and conflicts.

Keep Them Informed: Regularly update your investors on your business's progress. Transparency fosters trust and keeps them engaged.

Respect Boundaries: Maintain a professional approach to the funding relationship. Avoid mixing personal and business matters to keep interactions smooth and respectful.

Handling Challenges

Despite the advantages, seeking funding from family and friends can present challenges:

Emotional Pressure: The emotional stakes are higher when dealing with loved ones. Prepare for the additional pressure and manage it with sensitivity.

Potential Conflicts: Financial matters can create conflicts. Tackle issues swiftly and professionally to safeguard personal relationships.

Risk of Loss: Understand that if your business fails, it may strain your relationships. Be ready to manage this scenario with grace and responsibility.

Seeking funding from family and friends can be a viable option for starting your first business. By preparing thoroughly, communicating clearly, and managing relationships with care, you can effectively leverage this source of funding. Remember, the key is to approach the process with professionalism and respect, ensuring that both your business and personal relationships thrive.

CROWDFUNDING YOUR STARTUP IDEA

Crowdfunding has revolutionised the way entrepreneurs fund their businesses, making it an enticing option for startups. At its core, crowdfunding involves raising small amounts of money from a large number of people, typically via the internet. This method has gained popularity as it democratises the funding process, enabling anyone with a compelling idea to connect with potential backers worldwide. There are several models to consider. Reward-based crowdfunding allows backers to receive perks or products in exchange for their support, and it is popular on platforms like Kickstarter. Equity-based crowdfunding, on the other hand, involves granting investors a stake in your company. This model is more complex and is often used for larger funding goals.

Creating a successful crowdfunding campaign requires careful planning and execution. The story you tell is crucial; it must resonate emotionally with your audience. Think of it like a movie trailer: it needs to hook viewers quickly and make them care about the outcome. A compelling video can make all the difference. Show your passion, explain the problem you're solving, and demonstrate how your product is the solution. Setting realistic funding goals is another important piece of the puzzle. Aim too high, and you risk not meeting your target; aim too low, and you might not gather enough resources to truly make an impact. Establishing clear timelines helps manage backer expectations and keeps you accountable.

Choosing the right platform is crucial to maximising your campaign's potential. Kickstarter and Indiegogo are among the most well-known options, each with its own unique features. Kickstarter employs an all-or-nothing model; if you do not reach your goal, you do not receive the funds. Indiegogo offers greater flexibility, allowing you to keep whatever funds you raise, regardless of whether you reach your target. Take into account platform-specific requirements, such as campaign duration limits and video guidelines, along with fees associated with these services. Kickstarter charges a 5% fee on successful projects, in addition to payment processing fees of approximately 3–5%. Indiegogo's fees are similar but provide more options for fixed or flexible funding.

Building a community around your campaign is essential for success. Promoting before launch can help generate buzz and gather initial support before you go live. Begin by engaging with potential backers through social media and email lists. Share sneak peeks or behind-the-scenes content to spark interest. Once the campaign is live, maintaining momentum is crucial. Regular updates keep your supporters informed and invested in your progress. Encourage them to share your campaign within their networks; word-of-mouth can be incredibly powerful in reaching new audiences.

Engaging supporters doesn't end once your campaign concludes. Thanking your backers and keeping them updated on progress fosters a sense of involvement and loyalty. Consider offering exclusive updates or early access to new features as a token of appreciation. These gestures go a long way in maintaining strong relationships with those who believed in your vision from the start.

Interactive Element: Crafting Your Campaign Story

Outline three key aspects of your startup's story: the problem you are addressing, how your solution distinguishes itself, and why you are passionate about this venture. Use these points to craft a compelling narrative for your crowdfunding campaign video.

Crowdfunding is not just about collecting funds; it is about building a community that believes in your vision. The success of your campaign hinges on how well you can connect with potential backers and inspire them to invest in your dream. With thoughtful preparation and genuine engagement, crowdfunding can be a powerful tool to bring your start-up idea to life while fostering lasting relationships with supporters who share your passion.

ATTRACTING ANGEL INVESTORS AND VENTURE CAPITAL

When considering elevating your business, attracting angel investors and venture capitalists may be an essential step. These investors can provide the capital necessary to scale your operations, but it is crucial to understand who they are and what they seek. Angel investors are typically affluent individuals who invest their own money in early-stage startups. They generally look for ventures with high growth potential and a passionate founding team. Venture capitalists, on the other hand, are part of firms that pool funds from various sources to invest in startups, usually at later stages than angels. They seek scalable businesses with strong market potential and are often more involved in the company's strategic direction.

Both types of investors possess distinct expectations. Angel investors may prioritise a personal connection or passion for your industry, whereas venture capitalists often emphasise financial returns and market size. Understanding these differences enables you to tailor your approach effectively. Angel investors tend to be more flexible and hands-on with mentorship, while venture capitalists provide larger sums but expect rapid growth and stricter milestones.

Crafting a pitch that captures the attention of investors is an art in itself. An effective pitch deck should include essential components such as a clear value proposition, a comprehensive market analysis, and a persuasive financial forecast. Begin with a strong opening that highlights the problem your product solves, then elaborate on how your solution stands out. Present any sales or user data you already possess to demonstrate traction. When presenting, storytelling is crucial; investors need to connect with your vision. Be confident, yet also ready to answer challenging questions about your business model and future plans.

Your pitch isn't merely about slides; it's about engaging your audience. Practice delivering it until it feels natural and compelling. Consider presenting to peers for feedback, refining your message with every iteration. Authenticity and passion can make a significant difference, so allow your enthusiasm to shine through.

Connecting with potential investors necessitates strategic networking. Industry events and pitch competitions serve as platforms to showcase your startup and engage with investors face-to-face. These events are not solely about pitching; they are also about cultivating relationships. Follow up on connections made during such gatherings, as nurturing these relationships can lead to valuable introductions or opportunities in the future.

Online platforms such as AngelList provide another means to connect with investors. Craft an engaging profile that showcases your achievements and vision. Utilise these platforms to research potential investors, tailoring outreach to those who have expressed interest in similar ventures. Engage with investor communities by taking part in discussions or sharing insights on industry trends.

Negotiating investment terms can feel daunting, but it is essential to safeguard your business interests. Grasping term sheets is vital, as they delineate the conditions of the investment agreement. Pay attention to details such as equity percentage, vesting schedules, and control provisions. These aspects affect your ownership and decision-making authority within the company. Negotiation involves more than just securing funds; it is about discovering partners who align with your mission.

Common pitfalls include misvaluing your company or accepting terms that limit future flexibility. Seek advice from mentors or legal professionals when reviewing term sheets to ensure you are aware of potential red flags. Remember that while funding is essential, the right partnership can provide long-term strategic benefits.

As you navigate these discussions, concentrate on building trust with potential investors. Being transparent about your business's strengths and challenges fosters credibility, making them more inclined to invest not just financially but also emotionally in your success. Balancing assertiveness with openness lays a foundation for productive negotiation.

In this journey to secure investment, patience and persistence are crucial. Building relationships requires time, as does perfecting your pitch and negotiating favourable terms. However, with dedication and strategic networking, you can attract the right partners who believe in your vision and support you on your path to growth.

LEVERAGING SMALL BUSINESS LOANS AND GRANTS

Exploring funding options for your business can feel quite complicated and may hinder your ability to launch effectively. Small business loans provide a structured path with clear terms and benefits. Among these, certain loans stand out due to their attractive conditions and government backing. These loans address various needs, ranging from working capital to equipment purchases. Seek out loans that typically offer lower interest rates and longer repayment terms, which make them an appealing choice for many entrepreneurs. Microloans, on the other hand, are tailored to smaller funding needs and are often provided by non-profit organisations. They are designed to assist businesses with modest capital requirements. These loans are accessible to startups and small businesses that may find it challenging to qualify for larger loans.

Understanding eligibility criteria is crucial when applying for these loans. The application process for most loans involves demonstrating your ability to repay the loan through a robust business plan and financial projections. Microloans often require less stringent documentation but still demand a clear vision of how the funds will be utilised. Preparing a comprehensive application means showcasing your business's potential and your commitment to its success. This includes a detailed business plan, financial statements, and personal financial information. Lenders seek stability and a clear repayment strategy.

Business grants offer an alternative way to secure funds without the obligation of repayment. These grants are often accessible through government programmes, non-profits, or industry associations that target specific sectors or demographics. For instance, tech startups may discover grants aimed at innovation, while minority-owned businesses can obtain grants designed to promote diversity. Locating the right grant necessitates research and persistence. Start by examining government websites or grant databases that list available opportunities.

Writing a successful grant proposal requires skilful storytelling and attention to detail. Begin by understanding the grant's objectives and tailoring your proposal to align with those goals. Clearly articulate your business mission, its impact, and how the grant will help achieve your objectives. Highlight any unique aspects of your venture that differentiate it from others. Supporting your proposal with data or case studies enhances your case. Remember, grants are competitive, so distinguishing yourself is essential.

Building a strong credit profile is essential when seeking loans or grants. A solid credit score increases your chances of approval and can lead to more favourable terms. To enhance your business credit score, begin by ensuring all bills are paid punctually and maintain low credit utilisation. Regularly examine your credit report for inaccuracies and address any issues promptly. Keeping organised financial records is crucial; they demonstrate reliability and transparency to potential lenders or grant providers.

Managing loan repayments is a vital aspect of maintaining financial health. Start by creating a repayment plan that aligns with your cash flow. This plan should outline payment schedules, amounts, and any contingencies for unexpected expenses. Consistency in repayments builds trust with lenders and enhances your business credit profile over time. Avoid financial pitfalls by remaining vigilant about expenses and cash flow management.

Financial pitfalls can derail even the most well-intentioned businesses. Overextending on credit or failing to monitor cash flow can lead to unmanageable debt levels. To stay on track, regularly review financial statements and adjust budgets as necessary. Consider setting aside reserves for emergencies or unexpected expenses; this buffer provides peace of mind during challenging times.

In concluding this chapter on financing options, we have examined various pathways available to you as an entrepreneur seeking resources to fuel growth without compromising ownership or vision. From loans that provide structure to grants that offer opportunities without debt obligations, each option has its nuances but holds potential for those willing to navigate them wisely.

MAKE A DIFFERENCE WITH YOUR REVIEW

HELP SOMEONE ELSE START THEIR DREAM

"The best way to find yourself is to lose yourself in the service of others."

MAHATMA GANDHI

Helping others feels good. Even small acts, like sharing your thoughts, can make a big difference.

That's what this page is all about.

Just like you, there are people out there who want to start a real business. Not just a side hustle but something they can grow, take pride in, and maybe one day even pass on.

However, here's the thing… they're unsure where to start.

That's where **you** come in.

Your review could be the reason someone picks up this book and starts building their future.

My mission is simple:
Make business feel possible for anyone willing to try.

But to reach more people, I need your help.

Most readers choose books based on what others say. So, if this book helped you even a little, if it gave you a nudge, an idea, or even just a bit more belief in yourself, please leave a quick review.

It doesn't cost a penny.
It takes less than a minute.

And it might just change someone's life.

Your review could help...

- One more new business get started.
- One more parent support their family.
- One more young person choose a path with purpose.
- One more community gain a small business that makes a big difference.

To leave a review, just scan this QR code or go to this link:

[https://www.amazon.com/review/review-your-purchases/?asin=B0FC2T3D2N]

If you've read this far, I already know something about you:

You care.

And I appreciate that more than you know.

Thank you so much for your time, your support, and your belief in this mission.

Let's build something great together.

Stephen Brown

Author of *Start & Build a Successful Business*

CHAPTER 6
BUILDING YOUR BRAND IDENTITY

BUILDING a brand identity transcends the physical act of creating a logo or choosing a colour scheme; it is an intricate process of defining who you are, both fundamentally and aspirationally, and how you wish for the wider world to perceive you. The core of this process comprises your fundamental values, forming the underlying beliefs that inform and influence every decision your business makes, from the innovative products you create to the considerate ways in which you engage with customers. These values serve as an unwavering moral compass, illuminating your path as you navigate the complex and often uncharted landscape of entrepreneurship.

Envision a brand deeply rooted in innovation, perpetually pushing conventional boundaries while eagerly embracing new ideas.

Alternatively, visualise a business that prioritises integrity, upholding honesty and transparency in every interaction and transaction.

Some businesses may focus resolutely on being customer-centric, persistently ensuring that every decision made significantly enhances the customer experience.

These carefully chosen and well-defined core values not only serve to distinctly define your brand but also act as a beacon to attract like-minded customers who hold those beliefs dear to their hearts.

Upon gaining clarity on your values, it is essential to translate them into tangible visual elements that the external world perceives. A memorable brand logo serves as the face of your business, instantly recognisable and designed to convey your message swiftly and effectively at a mere glance. Partnering with a graphic designer can be an enlightening and enriching journey, one in which you diligently explore various concepts and ideas, gradually refining them until the optimal design emerges. This collaborative process involves providing the designer with clear and articulate guidance about your brand's ethos, personality, and desired aesthetic. Do not underestimate the profound power of colour psychology in this creative process; colours have the innate ability to evoke emotions and can substantially impact how your brand is interpreted and perceived. For instance, the colour blue often conveys a sense of trust and reliability, whereas the dynamic colour red can evoke feelings of excitement and passion.

As significant and impactful as visuals are, crafting a consistent brand voice is equally vital in establishing a cohesive brand identity. This voice embodies the distinct personality inherent in your communication efforts, whether through engaging social media posts, efficient customer service interactions, or compelling marketing campaigns. It should align seamlessly and harmoniously with your brand's core values, resonating profoundly with your target audience. Consider how different industries adopt diverse brand voices: for instance, a tech startup might favour a friendly, conversational tone intended to appear approachable and welcoming, while a luxury brand might choose a more sophisticated and authoritative voice to exude elegance and exclusivity. Aligning your brand voice with customer personas ensures that each communication feels personal, relevant, and relatable.

Establishing comprehensive brand guidelines is essential for maintaining consistency across all touchpoints and interactions. These guidelines serve as an indispensable rulebook for how your brand is represented to the world, covering everything from font choices and colour palettes to tone of voice and imagery usage. A meticulously crafted style guide acts as a valuable reference for anyone involved in creating content or marketing materials on behalf of your business. By consistently enforcing these guidelines, you prevent mixed messages that could confuse or alienate your audience. Consider it much like establishing the rules for a highly coordinated sports team where everyone understands their role, adheres to the same guidelines, and works together towards the same goal.

Interactive Element: Develop Your Brand Persona

Consider engaging in this enriching exercise to help clearly articulate and define your brand's identity:

- **Step 1:** Reflect deeply on your core values and thoughtfully list three that define your business unequivocally.
- **Step 2:** Brainstorm and outline inventive concepts for a logo that captures and visually represents these core values. You can prompt an AI design platform to help you create designs.
- **Step 3:** Jot down specific adjectives that effectively portray your brand voice (e.g., friendly, professional, sophisticated).
- **Step 4:** Draft essential elements for a style guide, including carefully chosen colour schemes, fonts, and other important visual components.

By diligently engaging in these exercises, you cultivate a deeper understanding of what makes your brand unique, and more importantly, how best to communicate that uniqueness effectively to others, ensuring that your brand resonates deeply with its audience.

CREATING A DIGITAL MARKETING BLUEPRINT

Creating a digital marketing blueprint is akin to mapping out your business's path in the bustling online world. It's not merely about throwing content out there and hoping it sticks. You need to establish clear, measurable goals that align closely with what you want your business to achieve. Consider these goals as the compass guiding your marketing efforts. It can be tempting to aim for the stars, but remember, it's about setting SMART goals: Specific, Measurable, Achievable, Relevant, and Time-bound. For instance, if you wish to boost website traffic, specify by how much and by when. Perhaps your goal is to increase traffic by 20% over the next three months. Metrics such as conversion rates or user engagement rates can serve as indicators of your success. These metrics function as checkpoints to ensure you're on track.

A multi-channel strategy is vital for reaching a broader audience. Imagine casting a wide net; each channel you utilise adds another strand that helps capture potential customers. Email, social media, and content marketing should function in harmony, reinforcing one another to create a cohesive message. Email campaigns can nurture leads with personalised content, while social media platforms engage audiences through interactive posts and updates. Content marketing, including blogs and informative articles, drives organic traffic and establishes your brand as an authority in your industry. Each channel has its strengths, and leveraging them ensures you don't miss out on potential customers who may prefer one platform over another.

Budgeting for digital marketing involves more than just allocating funds; it requires wisdom in distribution. Ad placements can quickly drain resources if not managed judiciously. Explore cost-effective methods such as using pay-per-click ads or leveraging social media's targeting capabilities to reach specific audiences without overspending. Striking a balance between paid and organic strategies is crucial. Paid advertising yields immediate results, but organic efforts cultivate trust and credibility over time. Allocate funds where they offer the greatest return on investment, ensuring you get the most value for your money.

Analytics are your best friend when it comes to measuring performance. They narrate the story of how your strategies are performing. Tools like Google Analytics provide insights into website traffic patterns, revealing where visitors originate from and what they do on your site. Social media platforms also furnish valuable data on engagement rates and the demographics of your audience. Utilise these insights to adjust and enhance your strategies. If a campaign isn't performing as expected, analytics can guide you towards the necessary adjustments.

Incorporating analytics into your strategy isn't merely about numbers; it's about understanding behaviour and preferences. Take the time to interpret the data. Which pages are visitors spending the most time on? Which posts generate the most interaction? These insights inform decisions that can enhance and refine your approach. Adjusting strategies based on data fosters a cycle of continuous improvement, ensuring that your digital marketing efforts remain relevant and effective.

In creating a robust digital marketing blueprint, remember that flexibility is essential. The online landscape shifts rapidly, and staying adaptable ensures you remain competitive. Regularly review your goals, strategies, and analytics to keep pace with changes and seize new opportunities as they arise.

Example of Digital Marketing Budget Allocation

Consider using a chart like this one to visualise where funds might go:

- **Social Media Advertising**: 30%
- **Content Creation**: 25%
- **Email Marketing**: 20%
- **SEO Optimisation**: 15%
- **Analytics Tools**: 10%

This allocation will depend on specific business needs and goals, but having a clear visual representation helps manage resources effectively.

Developing a digital marketing blueprint is not a one-off task; it is an ongoing process of refinement, learning, and adaptation. As you navigate the digital realm, allow clear goals to guide you, prudent budgeting to support you, and analytics to inform you. Remain flexible, and remember that each campaign presents an opportunity to engage more deeply with your audience.

MASTERING SOCIAL MEDIA FOR BUSINESS GROWTH

Navigating the intricate maze of social media platforms to astutely select the ones that best complement and enhance your business objectives is akin to mastering a revered art form. Each platform offers unique advantages and caters to distinct demographics, making it crucial for businesses to do their homework. Start with a comprehensive evaluation of where your target audience predominantly spends their time online. For instance, Instagram, the quintessential visual paradise, thrives on imagery and is perfect for brands immersed in the realms of fashion, food, travel, and other visually appealing industries. The vibrant usage of visual elements can turn ordinary showcases into compelling visual stories that captivate users. Meanwhile, LinkedIn serves as a sanctuary for B2B interactions, immersing users in a professional atmosphere where networking, industry insights, and thought leadership bloom. Younger audiences, on the other hand, flock to TikTok, the dynamic newcomer, offering a platform for inventive, often viral content that resonates with Generation Z. Choosing the right platform hinges on nuanced knowledge of your audience's demographics, such as age, interests, habits, and lifestyles. Consider which platforms align with your business objectives and evaluate where you can most effectively engage with your audience to foster growth.

The intricate process of crafting content that captures attention is a harmonious blend of science and art. Storytelling emerges as the indispensable secret weapon; it elevates ordinary posts to riveting narratives that strike a chord with your audience. Imagine each social media post as a page in your brand's book, an opportunity to weave a captivating tale. Consider the narrative thread that runs through your visuals, every image or video should tell a part of your brand's holistic story. Utilise compelling visuals to draw in the viewer's eye, making it nearly impossible to scroll by without pausing. Furthermore, user-generated content campaigns act as potent engagement tools. By encouraging your followers to share their first-hand experiences with your product, you nurture a sense of community and enhance brand loyalty through organic advocacy. Initiatives akin to Starbucks' "White Cup Contest", which invited customers to design their own cup art, not only rekindled user engagement but also resulted in a wealth of user-created content that essentially served as free advertising, amplifying brand presence with authenticity and creativity.

Building a steadfast online community goes beyond the routine act of regular posting; it nurtures authentic connections. Visualise your social media platforms as vibrant community centres, bustling with discussion and interaction, where individuals come together to engage, ask questions, and share experiences relevant to your brand. Live events, such as webinars or Q&A sessions, can significantly enhance engagement by fostering real-time interactions that generate excitement and provide followers with a tangible reason to return. Thoughtful responses to comments and messages not only demonstrate that you value your audience's input, but also cultivate an atmosphere of trust, encouraging further interaction and dialogue. An engaged, vibrant community often translates into a network of brand advocates who enthusiastically spread your message to a broader audience, thereby magnifying your impact.

Leveraging social media advertising is a shrewd strategy to broaden your reach beyond the limits of organic growth. Paid advertising provides the tools necessary to accurately target specific demographics, ensuring that your content reaches the intended audience at the right moment. Setting up targeted ad campaigns begins with establishing well-defined objectives, whether aiming for brand awareness, enhancing website traffic, or securing direct sales. Platforms like Facebook enable businesses to tailor their ads based on user interests and behaviours, creating an environment conducive to conversions. Retargeting strategies gently remind users about the products they've browsed but haven't yet purchased, nudging them back to your store, thereby significantly increasing the likelihood of conversion through subtle, targeted prompts.

The vast and dynamic world of social media presents a tapestry of endless possibilities for connection, growth, and innovation. By carefully selecting the appropriate platforms, creating engaging and captivating content, fostering an interactive and supportive community, and effectively leveraging the power of targeted advertising, you can harness social media's immense potential to elevate your business to new, unparalleled heights.

CONTENT MARKETING: TELLING YOUR BUSINESS STORY

"Facts tell, stories sell"

BRYAN EISENBERG

Crafting a content strategy is akin to planning a road trip. You require a destination, a map, and pit stops along the way. Your business goals serve as the destination, while your content strategy functions as the map guiding you there. Start by clearly defining what you want your content to accomplish. This could range from increasing brand awareness to boosting customer engagement. Once you have set your goals, it's time to plan your route. A content calendar is your reliable guide, aiding you in scheduling and organising content across various platforms. This ensures consistency and helps you monitor what's working and what isn't. As for the types of content, variety keeps things engaging. Blogs are excellent for sharing insights and establishing expertise. Videos can captivate audiences with visual storytelling, whilst podcasts offer a chance to explore topics in greater depth in an auditory format.

Creating high-quality content that resonates with audiences involves more than simply writing words on a page. It's about crafting a narrative that captures attention and evokes emotion. Begin with compelling headlines; they're the first impression your content makes. A great headline piques curiosity and invites readers to delve deeper. Once you have their attention, storytelling techniques breathe life into your content. Share experiences, anecdotes, or case studies that illustrate your points and make them relatable. Visuals and multimedia elements enhance your content, rendering it more engaging. Imagine pairing a well-crafted story with striking images or informative infographics. These elements help break up the text and maintain reader interest.

Optimising content for search engines is crucial in today's digital landscape. It's not just about writing for humans; you also need to consider how search engines perceive your content. Keyword research forms the cornerstone of SEO optimisation. This process involves identifying the terms your audience uses to search for information related to your business. Once you have a list of relevant keywords, place them strategically throughout your content, including in titles, headings, and naturally within the text itself. However, remember that keyword stuffing is unacceptable; it makes content cumbersome and difficult to read. Concentrate on integrating keywords seamlessly without disrupting the flow. On-page SEO best practices also encompass optimising meta descriptions, using alt tags for images, and ensuring your site is mobile-friendly.

Measuring content performance is not about vanity metrics; it's about understanding what works and what doesn't. Content analytics tools provide insights into how your audience interacts with your content. They track metrics such as page views, time spent on page, bounce rates, and social shares. These data points help you evaluate the success of your content efforts. For example, if a blog post has high page views but low engagement, it might indicate that the headline was effective but the content didn't deliver on its promise. Use these insights to refine your strategy and improve results. Constant monitoring and adjustments based on analytics ensure your content remains relevant and impactful.

Remember that content marketing involves sharing your story in a manner that resonates with your audience. It's not merely about selling a product or service; it's about forging connections and delivering value.

CHAPTER 7
MASTERING CUSTOMER ACQUISITION AND RETENTION

DESIGNING AN EFFECTIVE SALES FUNNEL

IMAGINE THIS: you're at a bustling market, where every stall competes for your attention. Each vendor has a strategy to engage you, spark your interest, and ultimately persuade you to make a purchase. This resembles a sales funnel, an essential tool for guiding potential customers from merely being aware of your business to actually buying. The sales funnel comprises four key stages: Awareness, Interest, Decision, and Action. In the Awareness stage, prospects first discover your product or service, typically through advertising or word-of-mouth. As they progress to the Interest stage, they begin researching and contemplating your offerings. During the Decision stage, they evaluate options and lean towards making a purchase. Finally, in the Action stage, they commit and complete the transaction.

Creating content tailored to each stage of the funnel is essential for nurturing prospects towards conversion. In the Awareness stage, content such as blog posts or social media advertisements can introduce your brand. As customers demonstrate Interest, engage them with informative webinars or comprehensive guides that explore your product's benefits. For those in the

Decision stage, case studies or testimonials can offer the reassurance needed to persuade them. At the Action stage, clear calls to action on landing pages simplify the purchasing process.

Consider utilising lead magnets, such as free resources like e-books or checklists that are offered in exchange for contact information to draw potential customers into your funnel. Landing pages should be optimised to effectively capture these leads. Once you have their contact details, personalised email nurturing sequences become crucial. These sequences provide valuable information tailored to each prospect's interests, encouraging them to progress further down the funnel.

Optimising your sales funnel involves analysing conversion rates at each stage and implementing improvements. A/B testing is a powerful method for refining elements like landing page headlines or call-to-action buttons. Small adjustments can have significant impacts on conversion rates. Conversion rate optimisation tools can help pinpoint areas for enhancement and monitor progress over time.

Automation plays a vital role in optimising your sales funnel. Marketing automation tools such as Mailchimp enable you to establish automated workflows that guarantee timely follow-ups with leads. These platforms can automatically dispatch personalised emails based on user behaviour, assisting in nurturing prospects through the funnel without the need for constant manual intervention.

MAPPING YOUR CUSTOMER JOURNEY

Create a visual map of your customer journey through the stages of the sales funnel. Begin by identifying touchpoints in each stage and listing the content or strategies you currently employ for engagement. Highlight areas where automation could enhance efficiency. This exercise will clarify where your funnel excels and where improvements are necessary.

By employing automation, you can concentrate on high-impact activities while still maintaining personalised engagement with prospects. For instance, establishing triggers that initiate email sequences when a lead downloads a resource keeps them engaged without necessitating constant oversight.

As you refine your sales funnel, remember that it is an ongoing process. Regularly review the analytics from each stage to assess performance and make data-driven adjustments. The goal is not merely to guide customers through the funnel but to create an experience that feels seamless and personalised at every step.

The art of effectively designing a sales funnel lies in understanding customer behaviour and needs at each stage. By crafting content that resonates with their journey and optimising touchpoints for conversion, you create a powerful system that attracts new customers and fosters lasting relationships with them. This approach ensures that your efforts in customer acquisition are not only successful but also sustainable in the long term.

CUSTOMER SERVICE EXCELLENCE AS A COMPETITIVE EDGE

In a world where most customers have countless options, exceptional customer service stands as a beacon that attracts and retains. We often hear the phrase "customer service," but what does it truly mean to excel in this area? At its core, exceptional service means anticipating and addressing customer needs before they even voice them. Imagine walking into a store and being greeted by someone who knows your name, remembers your past purchases, and offers personalised recommendations. That's the kind of service that leaves a mark. Proactive support practices, such as reaching out to customers to resolve potential issues before they escalate, can transform a one-time buyer into a loyal advocate. Personalised experiences, where customers feel seen and valued, build trust and foster long-term relationships.

Training your customer service team is crucial for delivering this level of excellence. Simply instructing employees is not enough; they require empowerment to make decisions swiftly. Role-playing scenarios are invaluable in this regard, assisting staff in navigating various situations with confidence. Imagine an employee dealing with an irate customer; role-play teaches them to defuse tension and offer solutions effectively. Empowerment derives from trusting employees to utilise their judgment rather than adhering to rigid scripts. When team members feel supported and capable of resolving issues independently, it boosts morale and enhances the service they provide.

In today's digital age, offering multi-channel support is no longer a luxury but an expectation. Customers wish to communicate through their preferred platforms, whether that's live chat for quick answers, social media for public engagement, or phone support for complex issues. Integrating helpdesk software ensures seamless transitions across these channels, providing a unified experience. Imagine a customer beginning a conversation on social media, continuing it via email, and concluding it over the phone, all without having to repeat themselves. This integration reflects an organisation that values customer time and convenience.

Measuring customer satisfaction is crucial for ongoing improvement. Tools like customer satisfaction surveys and the Net Promoter Score (NPS) enable you to gauge how well you are meeting expectations. These surveys provide direct insights from those who matter most: your customers. Once you have collected this data, the real work begins: using feedback to drive improvements. Consider a company that noticed low satisfaction scores regarding response times. By reallocating resources to reduce wait times, they not only improved scores but also enhanced customer loyalty.

Case Study: The Power of Feedback

A small tech start-up faced criticism for its lack of user-friendly interfaces. Rather than disregard the feedback, they engaged directly with users through surveys and focus groups. By implementing suggested changes, such as simplifying navigation and enhancing tutorials, they observed a 30% increase in customer satisfaction within six months. This case underscores the importance of listening to your audience.

Feedback should never be viewed as a one-off task; it is part of an ongoing dialogue with your customers. Closing the feedback loop involves making changes and conveying those changes back to your audience. When customers see their input valued and acted upon, it strengthens their connection to your brand. Transparency in this process fosters trust and demonstrates that you genuinely care about their experience.

Exceptional customer service is about more than handling complaints; it's about creating memorable interactions that make customers feel valued and understood. By defining what excellence looks like in your organisation, training teams effectively, embracing multi-channel support, and using feedback to fuel growth, you position your business as a leader in customer service excellence. This approach helps retain existing customers and attracts new ones through positive word-of-mouth, a powerful tool in any entrepreneur's arsenal.

BUILDING CUSTOMER LOYALTY PROGRAMMES

Crafting a customer loyalty programme can feel like piecing together a beautiful tapestry, with each thread representing a customer's journey with your business. Effective loyalty programmes are not merely about accumulating points or rewards; they are about fostering a connection and making customers feel valued and appreciated. At their core, these programmes offer a variety of rewards, such as points that can be redeemed for discounts, access to exclusive events, or even first choice on new products. Many successful programmes utilise tiered structures, where the more customers engage or spend, the greater the benefits they receive. It's akin to climbing a ladder, with each step offering more enticing rewards.

Personalising rewards is where the magic unfolds. Customers desire to feel like they are more than just another number. Tailoring rewards to their preferences can significantly enhance engagement and satisfaction. For instance, if you know a segment of your customers loves coffee, offering them a discount on their next cup can make all the difference. It's about paying attention to their likes and dislikes, using data to craft experiences uniquely suited to them. This personalisation can transform a regular transaction into a memorable interaction, strengthening the bond between your brand and the customer.

Once you have crafted these enticing programmes, effective promotion is key. A well-executed marketing campaign can showcase the benefits and excitement surrounding your loyalty offerings. Consider using email newsletters to announce new programme features or social media posts that highlight member stories. By sharing testimonials or showcasing success stories, you generate buzz and demonstrate the real-world impact of your programme. Imagine a post featuring a customer who used their points to attend an exclusive event—it's relatable and inspiring, encouraging others to join in.

ANALYSING LOYALTY PROGRAMME PERFORMANCE

Tracking and analysing the performance of your loyalty programme ensures it aligns with business objectives. It's akin to having a map; you might lose direction without one. Start by defining key metrics such as customer retention rates and average spending per member. These figures provide insights into your programme's effectiveness. For instance, if you observe an increase in repeat purchases after launching a new reward tier, it suggests that your strategy is working.

Data insights are invaluable for programme adjustments. Occasionally, you may need to tweak elements based on feedback or emerging trends. Perhaps customers prefer experiential rewards over monetary ones, such as exclusive workshops rather than discounts. Adapting your programme to reflect these preferences keeps it fresh and relevant.

A practical approach involves regularly reviewing programme analytics to identify areas for improvement. Utilise dashboards or analytics tools to visualise data trends and make informed decisions regarding potential changes. Consider conducting periodic surveys to gather direct feedback from participants. This input aids in refining offerings and ensures they remain appealing.

Promoting these updates to your audience is equally important. Transparency builds trust and demonstrates that you value their input. Communicate changes through various channels, whether it's an engaging newsletter or an in-app message, to ensure that everyone remains informed.

Loyalty programmes aren't static; they evolve alongside your business and customers' needs. Designing thoughtful, personalised programmes, promoting them effectively, and analysing their performance creates an ecosystem where customers feel appreciated and engaged. This approach fosters lasting relationships and encourages continued interaction with your brand.

Taking a moment to reflect on loyalty programmes reveals their potential for strengthening customer relationships. These initiatives offer tangible benefits and cultivate deeper emotional connections with customers, a powerful combination that drives long-term success. Your attention to detail in crafting these programmes can transform occasional buyers into brand advocates who champion your business at every opportunity.

UTILISING CUSTOMER FEEDBACK TO DRIVE IMPROVEMENTS

Customer feedback is the heartbeat of any business striving for growth and improvement. It provides direct insights into what your customers cherish, what they tolerate, and what they wish could be enhanced. Effectively gathering this feedback is paramount. Online surveys and feedback forms are straightforward yet powerful tools, enabling customers to share their thoughts at their convenience. Platforms like Google Forms or Survey-Monkey simplify the creation of questions that get straight to the point. Another approach is engaging customers in focus group discussions. This method fosters deeper conversations and uncovers nuanced opinions that might not surface in written responses. Imagine sitting down with a group of your customers and hearing firsthand what excites or frustrates them about your offerings.

Once you have this treasure trove of feedback, the next step is to analyse it for insights. This isn't just about numbers but finding patterns and themes that reveal customer needs and expectations. Sentiment analysis tools can be incredibly helpful here, as they sift through feedback to identify trends in customer sentiment, whether positive or negative. You might discover that customers consistently mention a particular feature they love or a common issue they're facing. Identifying these patterns helps prioritise areas for improvement. Trend identification goes hand in hand with sentiment analysis, allowing you to see how customer opinions evolve over time.

With clear insights in hand, it's time to implement changes. This step transforms feedback from static data into dynamic action. Consider a company that noticed customers frequently mentioning difficulties navigating their website. In response, they overhauled the site's layout to create a more intuitive user experience. Case studies like this illustrate the power of feedback-driven change. Techniques for prioritising these changes involve balancing impact and feasibility. Not all feedback can be addressed immediately, so focus on initiatives that offer significant benefits without requiring unsustainable resources.

Implementing changes is just one part of the equation; closing the feedback loop is equally important. Customers want to know that their voices are heard and valued. Effective communication strategies include updating customers on changes through newsletters or personalised emails. Inform them of what you heard and how you are responding. For instance, a restaurant might inform patrons that they have added new menu items based on popular demand. Transparency in this process fosters trust and loyalty, demonstrating to customers that their input directly influences business decisions.

ENGAGING WITH FEEDBACK

Take a moment to reflect on recent feedback from your customers. Consider the emerging themes and how they align with your business goals. Jot down one action step based on this feedback that you can take to enhance your customer experience.

Feedback is more than just a checkbox on your to-do list; it is a crucial element of continuous improvement. By effectively collecting, analysing, implementing, and communicating changes based on customer input, you foster a culture of responsiveness and innovation within your business. This approach not only enhances customer satisfaction but also strengthens their connection with your brand.

Remember that each customer interaction offers an opportunity to learn and grow. Considering feedback as a valuable resource sets your business up for long-term success in a constantly evolving market.

CHAPTER 8
MANAGING OPERATIONS AND PRODUCTIVITY

SETTING UP EFFICIENT OPERATIONAL PROCESSES

IMAGINE STEPPING INTO A BUSTLING KITCHEN, with chefs working seamlessly and harmoniously, each knowing their precise role in crafting the perfect dish. This visual metaphor embodies what efficient operations should aspire to achieve: a symphony of synchronously aligned processes working in concert. However, orchestrating such a balanced environment within your business does not happen overnight. It begins with a meticulous analysis of your current workflows, aimed at uncovering sources of delays and inefficiencies that may be quietly hindering your progress. In this analytical journey, consider yourself akin to a detective unravelling a mystery, identifying the pivotal points where tasks accumulate or where communication falters. Thoughtful use of process mapping tools serves as a critical resource. These tools translate abstract workflows into visual paradigms, much like cartographic maps or flow diagrams, thereby making it easier to pinpoint problematic areas.

In parallel, conducting workflow audits provides an additional layer of valuable insight. This approach involves observing the dynamics of workflow within your business as if you were an uninvolved observer peering through a window. During this observational audit, scrutinise the structure to identify redundant phases or consider whether tasks might be consolidated or wisely automated. When executed precisely, these audits can uncover surprising inefficiencies that tend to remain hidden amidst the daily narrative of business activities.

Once you identify the gaps, transitioning towards standardised procedures is essential. Standard Operating Procedures (SOPs) play a crucial role in ensuring consistency and quality, functioning much like a well-crafted recipe that guides your team diligently through each task. By systematically documenting the optimal way to complete each task, an operational framework is created that everyone can follow, thereby minimising errors and enhancing efficiency. For example, having an SOP for managing customer inquiries ensures that each team member provides consistent information, thereby enhancing customer satisfaction.

The development of SOP templates for routine tasks significantly simplifies this standardisation process. Imagine having a template for seamlessly onboarding a new employee, ensuring that no critical step, from setting up their workspace to integrating them into the team culture, is overlooked.

With standardisation, the journey towards operational excellence focuses on embracing continuous improvement. Methodologies such as Kaizen and Lean principles can be adopted, emphasising incremental modifications that accumulate to substantial improvements over time.

Consider implementing continuous improvement cycles where you regularly evaluate processes and propose innovative enhancements. These cycles can be as simple as a monthly team meeting where everyone is encouraged to share an improvement idea or a reflection on your business, asking yourself what would make it even better.

After each project, we hold a brief review, posing the question to ourselves:

"What Went Well? And, Even Better If?"

The training and empowerment of employees form essential pillars in maintaining streamlined operations. Organising workshops focused on process improvements can equip employees with the skills to identify inefficiencies and propose viable solutions. These sessions not only impart knowledge but also cultivate a sense of ownership and accountability among team members.

Employee suggestion programmes serve as another effective tool in guiding operational enhancements. Encouraging employees to share their observations and ideas allows you to utilise a reservoir of intrinsic knowledge that might otherwise remain untapped. Consider creating a platform where employees can submit suggestions anonymously, if they wish, thereby fostering an open environment conducive to innovation.

Workflow Audit Exercise

Allocate time to systematically observe your workflows. Identify any areas where tasks seem to slow down or where frequent clarifications are needed. Then, meet with your team for a focused brainstorming session to tackle these bottlenecks. Foster an environment of open discussion and collaborative problem-solving to uncover practical solutions.

By methodically establishing efficient operational processes, you foster an environment where productivity is not merely an aspiration but a thriving reality, and where creativity is not restricted but allowed to flourish. Each strategic step taken to refine these processes brings your business closer to that archetypal kitchen scenario: a modern enterprise where all components function with precision and shared purpose.

UTILISING TECHNOLOGY FOR BUSINESS EFFICIENCY

Technology is a dynamic force that revolutionises the landscape of business, especially concerning efficiency. It is a transformative experience to consider the vast amount of time and energy you could conserve by automating those tiresome, repetitive tasks that consistently drain your day. In today's fast-paced business environment, automation and AI tools have become indispensable allies in this ongoing pursuit of efficiency. Imagine a customer relationship management (CRM) system not merely as a tool but as a virtual personal assistant, diligently tracking every minute detail related to customer interactions, follow-ups, and opportunities for relationship-building. This complex yet user-friendly tool intricately organises your client data, offering valuable insights into customer preferences and behaviours. Such insights empower you to tailor your services more precisely to meet and even exceed customer expectations.

In a similar vein, automating invoicing and payment processes alleviates the monotony of tracking down payments and meticulously managing financial paperwork. With these automated systems, invoices are dispatched punctually, reminders are sent systematically, and follow-ups for late payments can be scheduled with minimal manual intervention. These tools ensure a steady cash flow and significantly reduce stress levels, allowing you to focus your energy on expanding your business, rather than becoming ensnared in administrative tasks.

Integrating software solutions can transform your operations into a harmonious ecosystem where each component functions in concert with the others. Imagine the seamless alignment created when your accounting software synchronises perfectly with your project management tools. This integration streamlines financial tracking and project budgeting, ensuring that every team member has access to up-to-date financial data, enabling informed decision-making at all levels. API-driven integrations act as the cohesive force that binds disparate systems together, facilitating effortless communication and data sharing between various software applications.

For example, by linking your CRM with your email marketing platform, customer data can flow seamlessly between systems. This sophisticated integration facilitates the creation of personalised marketing campaigns based on real-time customer interactions, significantly boosting engagement and enhancing conversion rates. By effectively dismantling the silos between various software solutions, you create a dynamic operational environment that is highly adaptable and continuously evolves with your business needs.

Communication is the true backbone of any successful operation, and technology has the potential to enhance how teams collaborate and interact. Implementing sophisticated collaboration platforms such as Microsoft Teams brings your entire workforce onto the same page, regardless of geographic location. These robust platforms facilitate real-time communication through chat, file sharing, and integrated project management tools, all within a single platform. It's akin to having an office without physical barriers—enabling everyone to contribute their invaluable ideas and insights at any time, fostering a collaborative culture.

Video conferencing platforms have become indispensable for organising remote meetings, effortlessly bridging geographical divides and nurturing a sense of connectedness among team members. Leveraging platforms like Zoom or Teams enables face-to-face interactions even when miles apart, ensuring that communication remains both personal and effective. These platforms help maintain a sense of team cohesion and ensure that everyone is aligned with overarching company objectives and goals.

Data analytics emerges as a powerful tool, offering insightful perspectives on every aspect of your business operations. Business intelligence (BI) tools effectively transform raw data into actionable insights, guiding strategic decisions with exceptional accuracy. Consider analysing sales data to identify clear trends: BI tools can pinpoint which products are performing well and which may need further attention. Embracing a data-driven approach enables businesses to make informed decisions based on evidence rather than mere intuition.

Consider how data analytics can significantly enhance efficiency in inventory management by accurately predicting demand patterns and optimising stock levels accordingly. By harnessing the immense power of data, you can effectively prevent overstocking or running out of popular items, thereby maximising profitability while minimising waste. Numerous examples of data-driven decision-making exist, from adjusting marketing strategies based on explicit customer feedback to optimising employee schedules according to peak productivity times.

Integrating technology into your operations is far from merely keeping up with trends; it's about creating an environment where efficiency thrives. By strategically utilising automation tools, implementing versatile software solutions, enhancing communication via cutting-edge technology, and harnessing data analytics, you establish a solid foundation for success that is both agile and robust. In doing so, you free up valuable time and resources, enabling you to concentrate wholeheartedly on what truly matters: developing your business and realising your entrepreneurial ambitions.

TIME MANAGEMENT STRATEGIES FOR ENTREPRENEURS

Time is an elusive resource, slipping through the cracks if not managed carefully. Prioritising tasks effectively becomes crucial when every second counts. Focusing on high-impact activities ensures that your energy is directed towards what truly matters. The Eisenhower Box is a powerful tool for this, helping you to discern between urgent and important tasks. Imagine sorting your daily tasks into four categories:

- Do it now: Urgent & Important
- Decide when to do it: Important & Not Urgent
- Delegate: Urgent & Not Important
- Delete: Neither Urgent nor Important

This visual guide can transform chaos into clarity, enabling you to prioritise the most pressing issues first. Another approach involves identifying key result areas, those pivotal aspects of your business that drive success. By concentrating on these areas, you can allocate your time where it delivers the greatest return.

In the bustling world of entrepreneurship, implementing time blocking safeguards against distractions and procrastination. This technique involves allocating specific time slots for various tasks throughout the day, establishing a structured schedule that promotes focus. Envision your day as a grid, with blocks dedicated to tasks such as meetings, creative work, and administrative duties. Setting up a daily time-blocking schedule demands discipline but enhances productivity. For example, reserve the mornings for deep work when your mind is freshest, and the afternoons for meetings or collaborative activities. Effective time-blocking practices may include leaving buffer zones between tasks to accommodate unexpected interruptions, ensuring that your schedule remains flexible and realistic.

Minimising distractions is a constant battle in today's digital age. Notifications ping incessantly, and the temptation to check social media lurks around every corner. Establishing a distraction-free workspace can significantly boost productivity. Consider designating a quiet area equipped with only the essentials: your computer, a notebook, and perhaps a plant for a touch of nature. Techniques such as setting specific times to check emails can help prevent constant disruptions. Additionally, apps like Focus@Will offer music scientifically designed to enhance concentration, creating an auditory environment that drowns out distractions and keeps your mind on track. We further enhance our office working environment with reed diffusers that provide aromas designed to improve concentration, increase energy, and reduce stress.

Utilising productivity tools can be a game-changer for efficiently managing tasks and meeting deadlines. The task management apps mentioned previously, such as Trello and Asana, are invaluable for organising projects and tracking progress. Imagine having a digital board to visualise tasks moving from 'To Do' to 'In Progress' and finally 'Done'. These tools not only keep you organised but also provide a sense of accomplishment as you witness tasks being completed. Digital calendars are equally essential for scheduling appointments and setting reminders. With colour-coded events and notifications, you can maintain a clear overview of your commitments, ensuring that nothing slips through the cracks.

While countless strategies may exist for optimising time management, the key lies in finding what resonates with you personally. Experiment with various techniques until you discover the combination that aligns with your work style and business needs. Prioritising effectively, blocking time, minimising distractions, and embracing technology are not merely strategies; they are lifelines in the demanding world of entrepreneurship. Once these techniques become ingrained habits, they guide your daily operations with unwavering precision.

TIME AUDIT

Spend thirty minutes over the next few days conducting a time audit. Record how you utilise each hour: productive work, breaks, and distractions. At the end of the week, review your audit to identify patterns and areas for improvement. Consider reallocating less important tasks to free up time for high-impact activities. This reflection not only helps refine your time management but also promotes self-awareness regarding your work habits.

By understanding and implementing these strategies, you establish a framework that promotes productivity and work-life balance, a crucial aspect often overlooked in the entrepreneurial hustle. As you navigate your business journey, bear in mind that mastering time management is not about cramming more into each day but about making every moment count.

CRAFTING A SCALABLE BUSINESS MODEL

Crafting a scalable business model relies significantly on your ability to establish repeatable processes. Review your product and service offerings and consider whether they can sustain an influx of growing demand over time. A genuinely great product should expand its reach with minimal disruption, seamlessly accommodating an increasingly large customer base without compromising quality or value. It is vital to evaluate whether your products can be easily standardised, adapted, or enhanced to meet shifting needs. There are instances where implementing minor tweaks or improvements can unlock a wealth of potential. Moreover, assessing market readiness is crucial. Is there an emerging or growing appetite for what you offer in the marketplace? Conduct a thorough analysis of market trends and consumer behaviour, diligently searching for patterns that suggest an impending rise in demand. The insights gained from this analysis will enable you to make informed strategic decisions about where to allocate your energy and resources most effectively.

Once you have identified scalable opportunities, building a robust infrastructure capable of adapting to growth demands becomes essential. The implementation of cloud-based solutions provides the flexibility necessary for seamless operational scaling. These solutions enable the expansion of storage and computing power without necessitating substantial investments in physical infrastructure, akin to the backbone that supports your business as it continues to grow. Consider examples of adaptable supply chain models designed to respond to varying demand levels. A flexible supply chain can efficiently ramp up production to meet peak demand periods while equally being capable of scaling back during slower times, ensuring both efficiency and cost-effectiveness. This adaptability is crucial for maintaining equilibrium between supply and demand, keeping operations smooth and unhindered as your business grows.

A critical component of scaling up lies in strategic financial planning for growth. Growing a business demands meticulous budgeting and vigilant cash flow management to avert financial strain caused by what is known as over-trading.

OVERTRADING: THE HIDDEN TRAP FOR AMBITIOUS BUSINESSES

In the early days of building a business, growth is exhilarating. Every new customer feels like a victory, every substantial order feels like validation, and momentum seems to be the ultimate goal. However, there is a hidden trap within that momentum that many early-stage entrepreneurs fall into: over-trading.

Overtrading occurs when your business outgrows its cash flow. You start to accept more orders, undertake additional projects, or attract more clients than your current resources, particularly your working capital, can support. On paper, you're "doing well." In reality, you're depleting your cash reserves, overextending either yourself or your team, and potentially heading towards a crisis.

Here's the irony: Overtrading doesn't initially appear to be a problem. It often resembles success. However, as your expenses accumulate, including stock, staff, deliveries, and contractors, you realise that the money flowing out is departing more quickly than the money coming in.

New businesses are especially vulnerable as they seldom possess substantial financial reserves or robust access to funding. A handful of late client payments, unforeseen expenses, or supply chain delays can send the entire system into chaos.

Red Flags to Watch For

- Sales are up, but cash is tight.
- You're constantly juggling supplier payments.
- You're extending yourself or your team beyond capacity.
- You're relying on short-term loans or credit cards to cover gaps.

How to Avoid It:

Overtrading isn't just a financial problem; it's a strategic one. Here's how to keep your growth healthy:

- **Know your numbers:** Regularly forecast your cash flow, not just your revenue.
- **Grow with purpose, not panic:** Say no to opportunities that stretch you too far, too fast.
- **Build financial buffers:** Aim for at least a few months' worth of operating expenses as a cushion.
- **Tighten your credit control:** Don't let overdue invoices stack up.
- **Prioritise profitability over vanity metrics:** Big sales numbers mean little if you can't pay your bills.

Begin by accurately estimating the expenses associated with scaling operations, which may include hiring additional staff, managing increased production costs, or enhancing marketing efforts to effectively penetrate new markets. Develop a comprehensive and detailed budget that accounts for these expenses while ensuring you maintain sufficient cash flow to cover ongoing operational needs. Techniques for managing cash flow effectively during expansion phases include maintaining a strategic cash reserve to address unexpected expenses, rigorous credit control, and negotiating favourable payment terms with suppliers. By proactively attending to your financial well-being, you can energise your business's expansion trajectory while avoiding common obstacles that may jeopardise growth.

I have always regarded our bank's relationship manager as a vital business partner. We hold regular meetings, and I send him our monthly management accounts so he can evaluate our performance. Should the business ever require a line of credit for an investment or unforeseen circumstance, our relationship is already established, and he is well-informed of our situation.

Monitoring and adjusting your business model will become an ongoing and essential process vital for sustainable growth.

Regularly assess the performance of your business model by utilising key metrics that provide insights into its current effectiveness. Metrics such as customer acquisition cost, customer lifetime value, and profit margins can highlight vital areas where timely adjustments may be necessary. Stay open to making strategic pivots when required to enhance scalability. For instance, if a specific product line is not meeting expectations, consider refocusing on products that demonstrate higher demand or profit potential. Numerous successful examples of strategic pivots include businesses that have redefined their offerings or explored new markets to seize emerging opportunities.

Early-stage entrepreneurship is a delicate balance between vision and reality. Growth is vital, but only if it is sustainable. Overtrading happens when ambition outstrips preparation. Stay grounded in your figures, manage your growth pace, and remember: real success isn't just about growing swiftly; it's about lasting long.

MANAGING RISK

Entrepreneurial risks are interconnected and can cascade into one another. A financial risk may trigger an operational risk, which in turn could lead to a strategic risk. Such ripple effects illustrate the complex web of challenges businesses face. Therefore, effectively identifying these risks and formulating strategies to mitigate them is crucial for ensuring the longevity and success of any enterprise.

Financial risks can abruptly disrupt stability, much like a rushing mountain torrent, leaving little time for a response. Unexpected cash flow shortages can arise from various causes, including macroeconomic upheaval (I've navigated my business through a recession, a credit crunch, and a pandemic!) or inadequate internal fund management. For example, late client payments may signal contractual issues or a broader industry slowdown. It is essential for businesses to establish robust financial monitoring systems and reserves that can absorb these shocks, akin to a dam designed to control water flow before it spirals out of control.

Operational risks often emerge as silent disruptors, manifesting through minor disruptions in day-to-day processes that have the potential to snowball into significant issues. For instance, a hiccup in the supply chain might begin with a single supplier's delay due to unforeseen strikes or geopolitical tensions. This minor setback can halt production and transport lines, resulting in a domino effect that can lead to a backlog and disgruntled customers. Therefore, diversifying supplier sources and implementing flexible logistics plans are crucial strategies, akin to constructing multiple roads on your mountain, ensuring continued access regardless of roadblocks.

Strategic risks arising from the shifting sands of market dynamics require businesses to remain agile and vigilant. These risks may arise from the emergence of a new competitor with an innovative approach, challenging your market position. Alternatively, they could stem from changing consumer preferences that render existing strategies obsolete. Companies that survive and thrive can swiftly pivot, adapt, and sometimes even lead these changes.

Compliance risks are equally pervasive. As businesses expand and operate across regional and international borders, they must navigate a labyrinth of regulations and legal stipulations, reminiscent of careful navigation along a trail to avoid treacherous cliffs. Failure to adhere to compliance can burden a business with hefty fines and reputational damage. Regular audits and training sessions for employees can act as guideposts, ensuring that each step taken is well-informed and precautionary.

Moreover, adopting tools such as risk assessment matrices promotes a proactive culture. In a dedicated risk identification workshop, encourage team members to identify potential vulnerabilities that may have gone unnoticed. By using a risk assessment matrix, you can visualise and categorise risks, aiding in prioritising them based on their potential impact and likelihood. This strategic approach ensures readiness for high-impact risks while remaining vigilant for smaller, albeit more frequent, disruptions.

The Risk Impact/Probability Chart serves as an essential tool. By systematically organising risks, businesses can establish effective priorities. Risks identified as high impact and high probability demand immediate attention and resource allocation. Low probability yet high impact risks should still be planned for, perhaps with contingency plans ready to implement at short notice.

Incorporating a SWOT analysis offers further clarity by providing an internal-external perspective. Internal strengths bolster your business against potential threats, while weaknesses reveal gaps that require reinforcement, such as an over-reliance on one key member of staff. External opportunities can inform your strategy, opening new ventures or collaborations, while threats, such as an over-reliance on one customer or supplier, might necessitate defensive manoeuvres.

It is essential to learn how to navigate these complexities and understand that risk management does not seek to eliminate all uncertainties, but rather equips you with the tools and insights necessary to manage them effectively. Acknowledge the uncertainties and embrace the proactive preparation that will empower your enterprise to remain resilient, regardless of the storms that may arise.

CREATING A RISK MANAGEMENT PLAN

Building a robust risk management plan is akin to piecing together a puzzle, where each component plays a crucial role in the larger picture. At its core, the risk management framework binds the entire structure together, guiding how you assess, manage, and communicate risks. Imagine it as the backbone of your strategy, ensuring that every potential threat is acknowledged and addressed. A strong framework encompasses risk governance structures that clarify how decisions are made. It defines roles within your team, assigning responsibilities to ensure everyone understands their part in managing risks. This clarity prevents confusion and helps align your team's efforts towards shared goals. Establishing a risk management team involves identifying key individuals who can provide diverse perspectives and expertise. These individuals may be internal or include trusted external advisors, who become your front line in recognising and responding to threats.

Once a framework is established, the next step is to develop strategies to mitigate these risks. Imagine you're weaving a safety net beneath a high-wire act. You want it to be secure, reliable, and robust enough to catch you if necessary. Diversifying your supplier base is one strategy that can buffer against supply chain disruptions. By not relying solely on one supplier, you reduce the likelihood of a single hiccup causing widespread issues. Financial hedging techniques also provide protection, acting as a shield against unpredictable market fluctuations. These measures serve as shock absorbers, softening the impact of unforeseen events. They represent proactive steps that enable you to navigate potential pitfalls with confidence.

Keeping an eye on evolving risks is crucial for any dynamic business environment. Regularly monitoring and reviewing these risks ensures that your strategies remain effective and relevant. This is akin to keeping your finger on the pulse of your business, ready to respond to changes before they escalate. Establishing regular risk review meetings creates a platform for open dialogue among team members. These discussions enable you to reassess existing risks, identify new ones, and adjust strategies accordingly. In today's fast-paced world, risk dashboards provide real-time insights into potential threats. These visual tools offer a swift overview of your risk landscape, helping you stay informed and make timely decisions.

Effective communication is crucial for aligning your team and stakeholders with your risk management plan. It is important for everyone to be on board and prepared to act when necessary. Clearly conveying your strategies fosters a sense of unity and readiness among stakeholders. Involve them in discussions to ensure their understanding and commitment. Approaches such as stakeholder engagement workshops encourage collaboration and allow stakeholders to express their concerns or suggestions. Including them in the planning process establishes a shared responsibility for managing risks. Communication templates can be invaluable tools for conveying complex information clearly and succinctly.

The significance of having a robust risk management plan cannot be overstated. It serves as a safety net that shields your business from unforeseen challenges and keeps you adaptable in the face of uncertainty. Successfully implementing such a plan necessitates careful thought, clear communication, and ongoing adaptation to changing circumstances. Establishing a comprehensive framework, defining mitigation strategies, monitoring risks, and effectively engaging stakeholders establishes the foundation for resilience and success in an ever-evolving business landscape.

As an entrepreneur, you will face various challenges and uncertainties. The risk management plan serves as your anchor amidst these storms, providing stability and guidance when it is most needed.

Creating an effective risk management plan requires careful planning and execution, yielding significant benefits by safeguarding your business against uncertainties while fostering confidence among stakeholders. By embracing proactive measures such as diversification strategies or financial hedging techniques, alongside continuous monitoring efforts using tools like risk dashboards or stakeholder engagement workshops, you will be well-prepared to navigate future challenges with resilience and agility at every turn.

CASE STUDIES IN PROBLEM SOLVING

In the world of business, challenges present themselves in various shapes and sizes, and the manner in which you address them can define your trajectory. Let's examine a tech company that faced a significant cybersecurity breach. This company was progressing smoothly until one day they discovered that their customer data had been compromised. Panic ensued; the stakes were high, with potential legal repercussions and loss of customer trust hanging in the balance. However, rather than succumbing, this company took a step back, assessed the situation, and sprang into action. They enlisted cybersecurity experts and utilised advanced analytics to trace the origin of the breach. It turned out that a vulnerability in one of their third-party integrations was to blame. By identifying the root cause, they patched the loophole and overhauled their entire security framework. Their response was swift and thorough, mitigating damage and restoring confidence among their users.

Another compelling example involves a retail brand navigating a significant product recall. Imagine launching a popular line of products only to discover defects that could harm consumers. The brand faced potential financial ruin and reputational damage. Yet, instead of concealing themselves behind corporate jargon, they opted for transparency. They implemented a comprehensive recall process, providing customers with clear instructions on returns and refunds. At the same time, their research and development team worked diligently to resolve the defect, ensuring future products met rigorous standards. The brand also initiated a communication campaign that educated consumers about product safety, reinforcing their commitment to quality. This proactive approach not only salvaged their reputation but also bolstered customer loyalty.

When analysing these scenarios, certain techniques stand out. Both companies employed root cause analysis, a methodical approach to identifying the fundamental issue rather than merely treating symptoms. They prevented future recurrences by investigating the underlying causes and implementing more robust systems. Additionally, design thinking played a crucial role, particularly for the retail brand. This human-centred methodology fostered creativity, enabling them to reimagine their product line with enhanced safety features while maintaining user appeal. Design thinking encouraged iterative prototyping and consumer feedback loops, ensuring that solutions were practical and aligned with market needs.

The lessons drawn from these case studies are filled with insights relevant to various business contexts. Timely decision-making emerged as a crucial factor during crises, highlighting the need for decisive leadership when each moment is significant. Prompt actions can prevent situations from spiralling further out of control. Cross-functional collaboration also proved invaluable; by leveraging diverse expertise within their teams, both companies developed comprehensive solutions that addressed multiple aspects of their challenges.

So, how can you apply these insights to your own business? Begin by embracing effective problem-solving frameworks. Root cause analysis is straightforward and can be tailored to suit various situations, whether you are uncovering operational inefficiencies or addressing customer complaints. It demands an analytical mindset and the readiness to explore deeper.

Design thinking provides an alternative pathway for innovation. This approach can be especially useful when crafting or enhancing new products. Motivate your team to think creatively and consider user experiences at each development stage. By cultivating a culture of experimentation and iteration, you establish an environment conducive to breakthroughs.

While frameworks provide structure, it's essential to customise solutions according to your specific needs. Every business is unique, with its own set of challenges and opportunities. Take inspiration from these case studies, but tailor strategies to suit your context. For instance, if your company encounters operational bottlenecks, focus on streamlining processes through automation or restructuring teams for greater efficiency.

Consider an interactive exercise: hold a brainstorming session employing design thinking principles. Identify a challenge, such as customer retention or supply chain disruption, and explore creative solutions.

The ability to pivot when faced with adversity can make all the difference in achieving long-term success. Embrace these real-world examples as guides on your journey towards building a resilient business that thrives despite challenges.

BUILDING RESILIENCE THROUGH ADAPTABILITY

Resilience in business is akin to a sturdy bridge spanning turbulent waters. It represents the capacity to withstand and thrive amid challenges, ensuring long-term success. But what cultivates this resilience? The answer lies in adaptability. When businesses adapt, they remain flexible in changing environments, much like a tree bending in the wind, yet never breaking. Consider companies that successfully navigated economic downturns. They didn't merely survive; they flourished by shifting their strategies, recognising new opportunities, and reimagining their operations.

Developing adaptive leadership skills is crucial for fostering a resilient organisation. An adaptive leader views change not as a threat but as an opportunity for growth. By empowering your team during uncertain times, you navigate challenges with clarity and vision. Techniques such as transparent communication, encouraging open dialogue, and building trust are vital. Consider leaders like Satya Nadella of Microsoft. By embracing cloud computing, Nadella led Microsoft through a significant transformation, revitalising the company's growth. On a smaller but equally important scale, during the Covid-19 pandemic, when most of our recruitment services were put on hold, Euro-Projects Recruitment pivoted to create a business forum where clients could network and share advice in uncharted waters, resulting in a community of customers becoming friends and long-term clients. These examples illustrate how adaptability and resilience go hand in hand.

Creating a culture of flexibility and innovation within your organisation is akin to planting seeds in fertile ground. A culture that encourages experimentation and embraces change fosters resilience by staying ahead of the curve. Encourage your team to think creatively, challenge norms, and explore new ideas without fear of failure. Innovation-driven companies often utilise techniques like brainstorming sessions and hackathons to stimulate creativity. Google's "20% time" policy allows employees to work on passion projects, frequently leading to ground-breaking innovations. Fostering a growth mindset among employees is critical; it encourages them to view challenges as learning opportunities rather than obstacles. This mindset shift propels innovation and keeps your business agile.

Continuous learning and development are vital components of building a resilient organisation. In an ever-evolving business landscape, remaining stagnant is not an option. Investing in training programmes and workshops ensures that your team remains equipped with the latest skills and knowledge. Consider companies like IBM, which invest heavily in employee development initiatives to stay at the forefront of technological advancements. By promoting a culture of continuous learning, you empower your team to adapt to new challenges with confidence. Encourage employees to pursue further education, attend industry conferences, or participate in online courses. These investments not only enhance individual capabilities but also strengthen your organisation's overall resilience.

Remember that resilience is not merely about weathering the storm; it's about emerging stronger on the other side. By fostering adaptive leadership, cultivating a culture of innovation, and prioritising continuous learning, you establish the foundation for a resilient organisation capable of thriving amid challenges. These elements work together harmoniously to create an environment where agility becomes second nature.

As Winston Churchill said:

"Never let a good crisis go to waste!"

CHAPTER 9
SCALING AND GROWTH STRATEGIES

RECOGNISING THE SIGNS OF A SCALABLE BUSINESS

SCALING A BUSINESS REQUIRES A NUANCED APPROACH. Not every business is prepared to scale, and recognising the signs demands a keen understanding of your current operations and market potential. Let's consider what makes a business scalable and how you can identify these key indicators in your own enterprise.

Identifying scalable business models begins with examining the core attributes that enable growth without proportional increases in cost. High-margin products or services often characterise these models. Such offerings allow you to expand your revenue significantly while maintaining relatively low costs. For instance, a digital product like software can be duplicated with minimal expense, unlike physical goods that require raw materials and manufacturing. Low overhead costs in relation to revenue growth further enhance scalability. If your business model enables you to increase sales without a corresponding rise in expenses, you're on the right track. This might indicate that you have already optimised systems or that you require only minimal additional staffing as you grow.

I set a goal to double the profitability of one of my businesses; it wasn't as straightforward as merely doubling the costs and turnover to achieve the same output; the sequence was something like this: Treble Costs, Quadruple Turnover = Double Profits.

To grow, we needed larger premises and office equipment, more support staff to care for the additional income-generating employees, increased training budgets, more expensive computer systems, HR management, and IT support. Scaling a business can exceed an optimal level, necessitating continual growth to achieve the next state of critical mass.

Assessing market demand and capacity is crucial in determining whether your business is ready to take the leap. Begin by analysing market trends. Are there shifts indicating a growing appetite for what you offer? Tools like Google Trends can provide insights into consumer interest over time. Beyond demand, capacity planning becomes essential. You must ensure your operations can handle increased volume without compromising quality or customer satisfaction. This involves evaluating your supply chain, production capabilities, and logistics. You're in a strong position if your current setup can comfortably scale up to meet demand spikes. However, investing in infrastructure improvements before scaling may be prudent if you anticipate bottlenecks.

Operational efficiency plays a vital role in successful scaling efforts. Start by examining your current processes, emphasising efficiency metrics such as inventory turnover rates. These figures can reveal how quickly you're moving through stock and highlight areas of waste or delay. Streamlining operations by eliminating redundant steps or automating repetitive tasks can free up resources. Consider implementing frameworks like Lean process improvements to enhance processes systematically. This prepares your business for scaling and instils a culture of continuous improvement, making future growth less daunting.

Evaluating financial health and stability is another critical step before scaling. A thorough assessment of your financial position ensures that you are not stretching your resources too thin. Key financial ratios such as the current, quick, and debt-to-equity ratios provide insights into liquidity and financial stability. A robust cash reserve serves as a safety net, offering flexibility and cushioning against unforeseen expenses during expansion phases. Maintaining an accurate cash flow forecast is also important, enabling you to anticipate financial needs and avoid potential shortfalls.

UNDERSTANDING KEY FINANCIAL RATIOS FOR A GROWING BUSINESS

As your business begins to grow, understanding and managing your financial health becomes increasingly crucial. Financial ratios are vital tools that provide insights into various aspects of your business's performance. In this section, we will explore some of the key financial ratios that every growing business should recognise.

Liquidity ratios measure your business's ability to meet its short-term obligations. The two most common liquidity ratios are:

Current Ratio: This ratio is calculated by dividing current assets by current liabilities. It indicates whether your business has enough resources to pay its debts over the next 12 months. A current ratio of 1 or higher is generally considered good, as it suggests that the business can cover its short-term liabilities with its short-term assets.

Quick Ratio (Acid-Test Ratio): This ratio is similar to the current ratio but excludes inventory from current assets. It provides a more stringent measure of liquidity. A quick ratio of 1 or higher is ideal, indicating that the business can meet its short-term obligations without relying on the sale of inventory.

Profitability ratios assess your business's ability to generate profit relative to sales, assets, and equity. Key profitability ratios include:

Gross Profit Margin: This ratio shows the percentage of revenue that exceeds the cost of goods sold (COGS). A higher gross profit margin indicates efficient production and strong pricing strategies.

Net Profit Margin: This ratio measures the percentage of revenue that remains as profit after all expenses are deducted. A higher net profit margin indicates better overall profitability.

Return on Assets (ROA): This ratio measures how effectively a business utilises its assets to generate profits. A higher ROA suggests more efficient use of assets.

Return on Equity (ROE): This ratio measures the return generated on shareholders' equity. A higher ROE indicates effective management and profitability.

Leverage Ratios: assess the extent to which your business is utilising borrowed funds. Important leverage ratios include:

Debt-to-Equity Ratio: This ratio compares total debt to shareholders' equity, indicating the relative proportion of debt and equity financing. A lower ratio is generally preferred, as it suggests less reliance on debt.

Interest Coverage Ratio: This ratio measures your ability to pay interest on outstanding debt. A higher ratio indicates a better ability to meet interest obligations.

Efficiency Ratios: Assess how well your business uses its assets and manages its operations. Key efficiency ratios include:

Inventory Turnover: This ratio measures how often inventory is sold and replaced over a period. A higher turnover indicates efficient inventory management.

Receivables Turnover: This ratio measures how effectively your business collects receivables. A higher turnover indicates efficient credit management.

In addition to understanding these ratios, you must also:

Analyse Cash Flow: Maintain an accurate forecast for upcoming quarters.

Build Cash Reserves: Ensure sufficient reserves for unexpected expenses.

This checklist serves as a guide for evaluating whether your financials support scaling efforts.

Considering these scalability aspects, remember that successful growth revolves around recognising opportunities while ensuring your business can sustain them. Whether refining your product offerings or enhancing operational efficiency, each decision should align with your strategic goals for expansion.

STRATEGIES FOR SCALING OPERATIONS

Scaling operations fundamentally involves a holistic and strategic approach that goes beyond merely establishing a robust business model; it requires devising and executing processes and systems capable of efficiently evolving alongside your growing ambitions. Consider your business a complex puzzle, where each piece, including systems, workflows, and resources, fits seamlessly together to create the larger picture. When formed correctly, this picture is a testament to your operations' strength and scalability.

Technology serves as a catalyst for scaling efforts, offering a range of tools designed to enhance your reach and capabilities without incurring significant cost increases. The rise of cloud computing solutions provides businesses with unprecedented opportunities for flexible data management. We have transitioned from a period of heavy investments in physical servers to an era dominated by system providers like AWS and Google Cloud. These platforms allow businesses to expand storage and processing power as needed, in response to demand. This dynamic scalability fosters business growth while mitigating the ever-present risk of obsolescence. Furthermore, automation, particularly in customer service, can completely transform customer interactions. AI chatbots handle routine inquiries, freeing human resources from monotony and enabling them to concentrate on more complex, value-added tasks. While these bots manage the mundane, your team can enhance the customer experience, which is crucial for maintaining customer satisfaction during growth phases.

Strategic partnerships emerge as pivotal players in scaling operations and broadening market reach. By collaborating with established distribution partners, one can significantly amplify market presence without requiring substantial investment in new infrastructure. These alliances facilitate the introduction of products to new audiences, allowing for the leveraging of existing networks to scale efficiently. Joint ventures offer an alternative yet equally powerful growth pathway. By partnering with another entity to penetrate an unfamiliar market, one effectively shares both the risks and resources involved, thereby accelerating entry without shouldering the full burden independently. Such ventures can also provide invaluable local insights and expertise, aiding in smooth transitions into new territories.

As your business scales, it is imperative that your workforce expands and adapts accordingly to meet growing demands. Expanding your team requires thoughtful and strategic hiring practices tailored to the complexities of rapid growth. Emphasise the recruitment of roles that directly contribute to your scaling objectives, focusing on skilled professionals who can deliver value from their very first day. Outsourcing non-core functions offers an adaptable solution for managing operational demands and alleviates the overhead associated with a permanent staff base. Tasks such as payroll or IT support free internal resources when outsourced to specialised external providers, allowing your team to concentrate on strategic initiatives and remain agile in an ever-changing environment. This allocation of tasks ensures that your core team stays focused and invigorated in driving growth.

As your headcount increases, it is essential to uphold your business culture and core values to prevent diluting what makes your enterprise unique and competitive. View each new hire as an opportunity to enhance and develop your culture.

Scaling is a multifaceted project that requires a delicate balance between internal optimisations and forming partnerships alongside technology adoption. Each strategy is tailored to serve a specific purpose, whether enhancing efficiency through ERP systems or extending market reach via strategic alliances. By addressing these critical areas with a comprehensive approach, you establish a robust foundation for sustainable growth. This foundation not only meets your current needs but also anticipates future challenges that may arise.

A meticulously planned expansion strategy must align with your long-term vision, ensuring that each decision is purposefully crafted to support your overarching goals without compromising quality or integrity. With effective strategies in place, scaling transforms from a daunting challenge into an exhilarating opportunity for growth and innovation within your business landscape, opening new horizons and unlocking higher levels of potential.

NAVIGATING GROWTH CHALLENGES

As your business grows, so do the challenges that accompany scaling. One of the most common hurdles is managing growing pains and operational bottlenecks. Imagine, for a moment, the pressure on your supply chain as demand surges. An unexpected rise in orders can quickly expose vulnerabilities, leading to delays and inefficiencies. These constraints may stem from suppliers struggling to keep up or logistical hiccups in transportation. To address this, consider diversifying suppliers to ensure a steady flow of materials. This approach mitigates risks associated with relying on a single source. Similarly, enhancing supplier communication can pre-emptively tackle potential issues before they escalate into production delays. Another technique involves implementing just-in-time inventory systems, which balance supply levels with demand, reducing excess stock and minimising waste.

Maintaining quality and customer satisfaction is vital during periods of rapid growth. The temptation to cut corners may arise due to an increasing number of orders to fulfil, but ensuring consistent quality must remain a priority. Implementing robust quality control systems is essential. Regular audits help identify weaknesses in the production process, allowing for timely corrections. However, these systems should not operate in isolation; they must be part of a broader feedback loop that directly involves customers. Encouraging customers to share their experiences provides valuable insights into potential areas for improvement. This feedback loop not only helps maintain quality but also fosters a sense of trust and loyalty among customers, as they see their input leading to tangible changes.

Addressing cash flow and financial management during scaling is another critical aspect that requires attention. As your business expands, so too do the financial pressures linked to increased operational demands. Optimising working capital becomes essential. Start by closely monitoring accounts receivable and payable cycles, aiming to shorten the former while extending the latter whenever feasible. This practice ensures a healthier cash flow by maximising available resources. Additionally, securing lines of credit can provide liquidity support during lean periods or unexpected expenses. Approach lending institutions early to establish relationships and negotiate favourable terms before you urgently require funds.

Adapting organisational structure to support growth is equally significant. As your business scales, the existing structure may no longer suffice. Restructuring becomes necessary to maintain efficiency and streamline operations. One effective approach is to implement cross-functional teams that unite individuals from various departments to collaborate on specific projects or goals. This arrangement enhances communication and problem-solving capabilities, ensuring that different parts of your organisation align towards common objectives. Furthermore, cross-functional teams promote knowledge sharing and innovation, as diverse perspectives converge.

Restructuring may also involve redefining roles and responsibilities within your organisation. As you grow, consider promoting from within to fill leadership positions, as these individuals already understand your company culture and processes. Alternatively, hiring experienced professionals from outside can introduce fresh ideas and perspectives that propel your business forward. Both approaches require careful planning but can enhance your organisational structure's adaptability and resilience.

Amidst these changes, maintaining open lines of communication is essential. Ensure that employees at all levels understand the reasons behind structural shifts and how these changes align with the company's long-term vision. Transparency minimises resistance and fosters a sense of ownership among team members.

These challenges offer opportunities for growth and learning when approached strategically. By tackling them directly, you establish a stronger foundation for your business's future and position yourself to flourish in an ever-evolving market landscape.

INNOVATING FOR SUSTAINED GROWTH

Innovation is often the beating heart of a successful business. It keeps a company relevant and ahead of the curve. Fostering a culture of continuous innovation involves creating an environment where creativity is not only encouraged but ingrained in the daily routine. Incentive programmes play a pivotal role in this. By rewarding employees for innovative ideas, you cultivate a culture where thinking outside the box becomes the norm rather than the exception. This could be as simple as recognising contributions in team meetings or offering bonuses for ideas that lead to tangible improvements. Moreover, consider establishing innovation labs within your organisation. These dedicated spaces allow employees to experiment with new concepts without the fear of failure. It is like having a playground where ideas can run free and transform into viable solutions.

Exploring new products and market opportunities is another way to sustain growth. The business world is dynamic, and those who adapt thrive. Techniques for market diversification, such as entering new demographics or geographic regions, can provide fresh revenue streams. It is essential to stay attuned to consumer trends and needs, which can highlight areas ripe for expansion. Meanwhile, prototyping and testing new product ideas allows you to refine concepts before full-scale production. This iterative process saves resources and ensures that what you launch resonates with your audience. Remember, sometimes the most unexpected ideas become game-changers, so never shy away from exploring uncharted territories.

Investing in research and development (R&D) may seem a luxury reserved for large corporations, but it is essential for any business that aims to remain competitive. Allocating resources to R&D initiatives is akin to planting seeds for future innovations. It necessitates dedicating time, talent, and budget to explore new technologies, enhance existing products, or even create entirely new offerings. This investment not only keeps your business at the cutting edge of industry advancements but also demonstrates to stakeholders that you are committed to long-term growth. In an era where technology evolves rapidly, remaining stagnant can lead to falling behind.

Alternatively, you can always seek innovations in your market that you can harness to your advantage. Around the time Euro Projects Recruitment was founded, the early emergence of online job boards was also taking place; forming a strategic alliance with the leading job board in our industry enabled our business to grow exponentially alongside this new technology, outpacing more established direct competitors who were slow to recognise this shift in the market.

Leveraging customer insights for innovation is one of the most powerful strategies available to you. Your customers are a wealth of information, providing real-world perspectives on what works and what doesn't. Customer journey mapping offers a detailed overview of their experiences and interactions with your brand. This visualisation can reveal pain points and opportunities you may have overlooked. Beyond mapping, consider co-creation initiatives with key customers. Invite them into the innovation process, seeking their input on product development or service enhancements. This collaboration not only strengthens customer relationships but also ensures that what you create aligns with their needs.

ATTRACTING TALENT:

Today, your business may exist only as a concept. Now, picture entering a room filled with talented, eager, and enthusiastic individuals, all working together to turn your vision into reality, an aspiration for many entrepreneurs who recognise the growth and dynamism that such a team could bring.

Yet, achieving this dream requires a blend of strategy, insight, and finesse, beginning with a clear organisational chart that outlines your roles, supported by compelling job descriptions that resonate profoundly with potential candidates. Identifying key roles and responsibilities is an essential step in this process. Envision not merely an organisational chart, but a team with shared values, specialised competencies, skills, and potential, where each thread plays a critical role.

Understanding the crucial roles begins with assessing your company's core objectives and mission-centred goals. These roles do not merely fill a position on paper; they form the backbone of your operations, directly influencing your business's trajectory. Consider the unique skills and qualifications that will propel your company forward. Reflect on the daily, weekly, and monthly tasks essential for the smooth operation of your enterprise. This is not simply about checking tasks off a list; it is about crafting roles that synergise and complement your overarching business aspirations, ensuring alignment with long-term goals and strategies.

Many entrepreneurs believe they need to clone themselves to grow their businesses, when in reality, what they require is someone who is the exact opposite to manage all the critical tasks they dislike or struggle with. Consider that many entrepreneurs have built their businesses by handling most of the sales; they understand their best customers and what the market demands. In such cases, this business owner likely needs someone who can oversee production or back-office activities, thereby freeing up time for them to acquire and expand their customer base.

ROLE PROFILES:

Creating role profiles is not a bureaucratic chore; quite the opposite. It presents a strategic opportunity to define and attract the right talent by reflecting your company's ethos and brand personality. Using engaging language that mirrors your dynamic company culture can set you apart. Be transparent about what you expect from candidates, providing them with a glimpse of what they can anticipate in return. Beyond merely listing responsibilities, illustrate a vivid image of what life at your company is like. Examine how leading companies, such as Google or Zappos, structure their job descriptions. These firms are renowned for including sections that describe their unique work environment and the types of employees who thrive there, creating a compelling vision that appeals to potential candidates.

Every Role Profile should begin with a clear explanation of the job's purpose and what it is ultimately intended to achieve.

This should be supported by the key outcomes this role must deliver to be successful. Whenever I discuss a new role with a customer, I always ask, "Imagine you are sitting with this person one year from now and they have exceeded all expectations, what would they have done for that to be so?"

Next, your Role Profile must include the key competencies expected of a high-level performer in this role. Training someone is always easier when they possess an innate ability for that skill within their behavioural profile. For instance, if someone is creative and enjoys art and design, they will naturally gravitate towards a role that allows these interests to be exercised.

Once you have meticulously crafted these compelling roles, focus on the strategic dissemination of these opportunities. Utilise career platforms and networking systems effectively to reach a wider audience, ensuring you attract a diverse and qualified pool of candidates. Platforms like LinkedIn, Indeed, and Glassdoor become indispensable allies, offering pathways to target specific demographics and industry professionals who are actively seeking new opportunities. However, do not confine your search to the digital realm. Networking events, industry conferences, and local business meet-ups provide invaluable connections, allowing for face-to-face interactions with potential hires, offering a more human touch than an online résumé can provide.

Fostering diversity and inclusion isn't merely a corporate check-box; it is an essential component in building a vibrant and innovative team. It's vital to craft job advertisements that resonate with a wide array of candidates. Use language that is inclusive and inviting, encouraging individuals from various backgrounds to apply. Clearly demonstrate your company's commitment to diversity, highlighting any initiatives that reinforce this focus. For instance, look to companies like Intel, which have implemented targeted programmes to enhance diversity within their teams, resulting in workplaces that are not only more innovative but also more resilient and adaptable.

CRAFT YOUR JOB DESCRIPTION

Now, take a pause and engage in this interactive exercise by drafting a job description for a position you're looking to fill within your organisation. Begin by creating the job title and defining its overall purpose before listing its key responsibilities and necessary qualifications. Reflect thoughtfully on how this role integrates with your business's objectives and enhances its attractiveness as an employment destination. This exercise is essential not only for articulating the vital role each position plays but also for ensuring alignment with your organisational values and mission.

As you prepare to welcome new talent into your organisation, remember that crafting job descriptions involves more than simply enumerating tasks. It requires defining roles that resonate with your vision and values, ensuring that you attract individuals who not only meet the job's requirements but also embody the spirit and ethos of your company. Clarity, creativity, and a commitment to fostering an inclusive culture are pivotal in this endeavour. Through deliberate and thoughtful planning and execution, you can build a team that not only meets immediate organisational needs but also drives your business toward a more robust and prosperous future. This approach nurtures an environment where innovation thrives, and your company's aspirations are met with dynamic and collective momentum.

Interviewing and Selecting the Right Candidates

Bringing new talent into your business is not merely an exercise in filling vacant positions but a pivotal step in shaping the future of your organisation. The interview process, therefore, becomes a critical tool in your hiring arsenal, one that must be carefully crafted to identify not only technical skills but also to ensure alignment with your organisational goals. This isn't just about asking a set of predefined questions; rather, it's about creating a structured framework that facilitates a deeper understanding of whether a candidate truly fits your business needs.

Begin by crafting a clear framework for your interviews, serving as the foundation for consistency, fairness, and efficiency. This structure should encompass a comprehensive list of key questions meticulously aligned with the specific skills, experiences, and attributes you seek. These questions act as your compass, guiding the conversation to focus on areas that are of utmost importance to your business's current and future objectives. It is crucial to ensure that every individual question ties back to the fundamental responsibilities and expectations of the role, thereby enabling you to effectively evaluate a candidate's aptitude to meet those demands.

THE POWER OF BEHAVIOURAL INTERVIEWS

Behavioural interviews emerge as a vital method for revealing how potential hires might perform in real-world scenarios. By exploring past experiences, you can gain deep insights into how candidates have navigated challenges and seized opportunities, often serving as a reliable predictor of future performance. When conducting these interviews, it is advantageous to ask candidates to share specific situations where they demonstrated key skills or overcame obstacles. This approach not only highlights their capabilities but also provides an intimate view into their problem-solving processes, decision-making skills, and resilience. For instance, posing questions like, "Can you recount a time when you faced a significant challenge at work and how you navigated the resolution?" offers a window into their technical skills and interpersonal prowess, which are vital for thriving within your company's distinctive culture.

EVALUATING CULTURAL FIT AND BEYOND

Assessing candidates transcends merely evaluating their resumes or parsing through their interview responses. It fundamentally involves gauging how well they integrate with your company's values and culture. This cultural synergy is often as pivotal as any technical prowess they might exhibit. To effectively gauge this alignment, it is crucial to weave assessments that reflect your company's ethos into the broader evaluation process. Practical tests and assessment tools can be immensely beneficial here, providing a more objective measure of a candidate's genuine abilities. If collaboration is a core organisational value, consider incorporating group activities during the interview process to observe firsthand how candidates engage with others. This approach offers a real-time evaluation of their teamwork acumen and communication style. Additionally, implementing personality assessments or cultural alignment questionnaires can underscore how seamlessly they align with your organisational values and ethos.

DECISION-MAKING - THE FINAL STEP

Once you have gathered all relevant information, making the final hiring decision requires a balanced, methodical approach. Decision matrices can be incredibly beneficial in this context, enabling you to systematically compare candidates across a range of criteria. By listing each candidate's strengths and weaknesses in relation to your prioritised requirements, you can effectively visualise who best meets your needs. Moreover, this method promotes a more impartial decision-making process, reducing the influence of personal biases that might inadvertently arise. When the time comes to extend an offer, negotiation becomes a key stage. Approaching this phase with transparency and flexibility is essential, ensuring that both parties feel adequately valued and heard. Effective negotiation tactics should include discussions not just about salary but also about benefits, career growth opportunities, and work-life balance considerations—factors that hold increasing importance for today's workforce.

Throughout this meticulous process, it is crucial to remember that each step, from preparation to the final offer, should cohesively reflect your company's values and culture. This consistency not only attracts candidates who resonate with your mission but also sets a positive tone for their future experience within your organisation. As you refine your interviewing strategy, it becomes clear that it is about more than just filling a position; it is about evolving a team that can propel your business forward with visionary passion and unwavering purpose. By focusing on thoughtful strategy, comprehensive evaluation, and strategic decision-making, you will be well-equipped to select candidates who will contribute meaningfully to your company's sustained success and growth trajectory.

CREATING A POSITIVE COMPANY CULTURE

Cultivating a positive company culture is akin to nurturing a garden where each plant flourishes in unison, enhancing the ecosystem. This starts with defining your company's core values —those guiding principles that shape behaviour and decision-making. Visualise these values as the roots of your organisation, anchoring everything securely. Whether it's transparency, collaboration, or innovation, these values must resonate with both you and your team. To effectively convey them, incorporate these principles into daily practices. It's not about plastering slogans on walls but about embodying those principles in every interaction and decision. For instance, if transparency is a core value, ensure open access to information across the board. Establish channels for employees to express their opinions freely, fostering an environment where everyone feels heard and valued.

Open communication serves as the lifeblood of any successful organisation. It's the bridge that connects ideas, resolves conflicts, and fosters innovation. Regular team meetings and feedback sessions can nurture this openness. These gatherings aren't meant to be mere formalities; they should be environments where honest dialogue thrives. Encourage your team to share thoughts and ideas without fear of judgement. Utilise communication platforms like Slack for more informal interactions, breaking down barriers and keeping everyone informed. This digital space can act as a virtual water cooler, where spontaneous conversations ignite creativity and camaraderie.

When we discuss employee engagement and well-being, consider it as the sunshine that nurtures growth in your organisational garden. Happy employees are more productive, creative, and committed. Offer flexible work arrangements to accommodate diverse needs and lifestyles. This flexibility empowers employees to balance work with personal commitments, thereby reducing stress and enhancing overall satisfaction. Think about introducing wellness programmes that promote physical and mental health. This could include yoga classes, mindfulness workshops, or even a simple initiative to encourage regular breaks throughout the workday. These programmes demonstrate that you value your team's well-being beyond their professional contributions.

Recognising and rewarding performance is akin to watering your plants—crucial for sustained growth. Recognition isn't just about handing out bonuses or plaques; it's about acknowledging efforts in ways that resonate personally with each individual.

Implement recognition programmes that celebrate both small wins and significant achievements. A simple "thank you" or a shoutout during team meetings can significantly boost morale. For high performers, consider tailored reward systems that align with their preferences and motivations. This might involve offering opportunities for professional development or experiences that they find personally fulfilling. The key is to make recognition meaningful and authentic.

One approach to embedding these practices in your company culture involves creating rituals or traditions that reinforce core values and foster a sense of belonging. For example, you might start meetings with a brief round of gratitude or end the week with a casual team gathering where everyone can unwind and connect on a personal level. These rituals not only strengthen relationships but also serve as reminders of what your company stands for.

Another important aspect of creating a positive culture is fostering inclusivity. Celebrate diversity by acknowledging various perspectives and experiences within your team. Encourage collaboration across departments and hierarchies, ensuring that everyone has a voice in decision-making processes. This inclusivity fuels innovation by uniting diverse viewpoints to address challenges from multiple angles.

As your company grows, maintaining this positive culture requires ongoing effort and reflection. Regularly revisit your core values to ensure they remain relevant and aligned with your evolving goals. Solicit feedback from employees on how well these values are being upheld within the organization—this not only provides valuable insights but also empowers employees to take ownership of the culture they're part of.

Visualise your company as a thriving ecosystem where every individual plays an integral role in nurturing its success. By defining clear values, promoting open communication, prioritising well-being, recognising performance, and fostering inclusivity, you create an environment in which both people and ideas flourish together harmoniously.

Remember that culture is not static; it is dynamic and ever-evolving based on interactions among people within your organisation. Remain attuned to shifts in dynamics or emerging challenges so you can adapt proactively while staying true to your foundational principles.

In this vibrant garden of possibilities lies the potential for growth beyond measure, growth both in terms of profits and human connection, creativity, and fulfilment that ultimately drives long-term success for both individuals and the organisation as a whole.

LEADERSHIP SKILLS FOR FIRST-TIME ENTREPRENEURS

Understanding and developing emotional intelligence is crucial for anyone stepping into a leadership role. It involves more than merely managing a team; it encompasses understanding them as well. Emotional intelligence begins with self-awareness, a clear perception of your emotions, strengths, weaknesses, and how they affect others. It's not just a buzzword but a tool that helps you connect with your team, fostering an environment where everyone feels valued and heard. Start by reflecting on your reactions to various situations. Journaling can be beneficial; write down what triggered certain emotions and how you addressed them. This introspection enhances self-awareness, steering you towards improved emotional regulation. Empathy, another cornerstone of emotional intelligence, enables you to see things from your team's perspective. Practise active listening by giving your full attention during conversations, asking questions, and showing genuine interest in their concerns. These skills help your team feel understood and respected, promoting trust and collaboration.

Building trust and credibility with your team is vital for effective leadership. It's not something you can demand; it's something you earn through consistent actions and integrity. Leading by example is crucial here. Show up on time, meet deadlines, and hold yourself accountable, just as you expect from your team. Consistency in actions creates a strong foundation of trust over time. Take, for instance, leaders like Warren Buffett, who inspire trust through transparency and ethical practices. His consistency in values and decision-making has fostered a culture of trust within his organisations. Trust is the glue that binds teams together, enabling open communication and collaboration. When your team trusts you, they are more likely to take risks, share ideas, and work towards common goals with enthusiasm.

When it comes to decision-making and problem-solving, having a structured approach can make all the difference. Decision-making doesn't occur in isolation; it thrives on collaboration. Engage your team by seeking their input and perspectives before making significant decisions. This inclusion strengthens the team's commitment to the outcome and often leads to more innovative solutions. Use techniques such as brainstorming sessions or collaborative workshops to harness collective wisdom. Problem-solving requires creativity, so encourage your team to think outside the box, exploring unconventional solutions to challenges. Look at companies like Google, where innovation stems from an environment that fosters creative problem-solving. Their approach to allowing employees time for personal projects has led to incredible breakthroughs and innovations.

Adapting your leadership style to meet the diverse needs of your team is essential for fostering growth and development. Not everyone responds in the same way to a particular leadership approach. The situational leadership model suggests adjusting your style based on the maturity and competence of your team members. Some may require more guidance and support, while others thrive with autonomy, recognising these differences helps you tailor your approach effectively. Leaders such as Satya

Nadella of Microsoft exemplify adaptability by encouraging a culture of learning and curiosity, allowing team members to grow in ways that align with their strengths and interests. This adaptability not only empowers individuals but also enhances overall team performance.

As we conclude this chapter on leadership skills for first-time entrepreneurs, remember that leadership is not merely about directing; it is also about inspiring and empowering those around you. By developing emotional intelligence, building trust, refining decision-making skills, and adapting your leadership style, you lay the groundwork for a thriving team that propels your business forward. These skills are not only pivotal for effective leadership but also in nurturing a culture where everyone feels valued and engaged.

CHAPTER 10
CONTINUOUS LEARNING AND ADAPTATION

EMBRACING A GROWTH-ORIENTED MINDSET

EMBARKING on the entrepreneurial path is akin to learning a new language. Initially, it feels overwhelming, filled with strange words and unfamiliar customs. However, as you delve deeper, the pieces begin to fit together, and your fluency improves. This parallels adopting a growth-oriented mindset, where every experience transforms into an opportunity to learn and grow. Unlike a fixed mindset, which perceives abilities as static, a growth mindset embraces challenges as avenues for development. It involves viewing setbacks as springboards for future success.

Picture this: an entrepreneur who views a failed product launch not as a defeat, but as an opportunity to gather insights and refine their approach. They see each challenge not as a road-block, but as a stepping stone. This mindset isn't just theoretical; it's embodied by successful entrepreneurs who continually adapt and evolve. Take Elon Musk, for example. His journey through multiple industries, from software to space exploration, demonstrates his commitment to learning from every experience, whether triumph or failure. This relentless pursuit of growth distinguishes those who merely survive from those who truly thrive.

Cultivating growth-oriented habits requires intentional effort. Start by practising self-reflection regularly. Take time to analyse your experiences, identifying what went well and where there is room for improvement. This introspection allows you to learn from failures without dwelling on them. Set learning goals alongside your business objectives, and commit to acquiring new skills or knowledge that can propel your venture forward. Perhaps you aim to master digital marketing or enhance your leadership capabilities; these goals nurture personal and professional advancement.

Recognising and challenging limiting beliefs is crucial for personal growth. These beliefs often lurk in our subconscious, whispering doubts that hinder progress. Cognitive reframing offers a powerful technique for transforming these negative thoughts into empowering affirmations. When faced with self-doubt, reframe it into a positive statement: instead of thinking, "I can't handle this," shift to "I'm capable of finding solutions." Journaling exercises can aid this process by providing a space for self-discovery and reflection. Write about moments when you've overcome challenges, reinforcing that you're equipped to tackle whatever comes your way.

Fostering a culture of growth within your organisation amplifies its impact. Encourage team members to adopt growth-oriented mindsets by implementing team-wide learning initiatives. Host workshops where employees can explore new skills or collaborate on innovative projects. These initiatives enhance individual capabilities and strengthen the team as a whole. Consider organising team growth challenges, friendly competitions that promote skill-building and creative problem-solving.

One instance of nurturing team growth is the concept of "hackathons." These events provide opportunities for teams to brainstorm and develop solutions within a short timeframe, encouraging creativity and innovation. By tackling these challenges together, teams cultivate camaraderie and promote a culture of continuous improvement.

Reflection Exercise

Take a moment for introspection. Grab a notebook and jot down the recent challenges you've encountered in your business journey. Reflect on how you approached them. Did you view them as insurmountable obstacles or as opportunities for growth? Consider how adopting a growth mindset might have changed your perspective or outcomes. What lessons have you learnt from these experiences? Use this exercise to reinforce your commitment to growth and adaptability.

Remember that cultivating a growth-oriented mindset is an ongoing journey rather than a destination. It involves continuously challenging yourself, embracing uncertainty, and viewing every experience, whether good or bad, as an opportunity to learn and evolve. As you continue to navigate the entrepreneurial landscape, let this mindset guide you towards new horizons filled with possibility and potential.

Through self-reflection, intentional habit-building, and cultivating a culture of growth within your team, you will unlock new levels of resilience and innovation. These strategies enhance your ability to adapt and thrive in an ever-evolving business landscape. Embrace the challenges ahead with enthusiasm, knowing that each step forward brings you closer to realising your full potential as an entrepreneur.

LEVERAGING NETWORKING AND MENTORSHIP

In the realm of business, connections are currency. I always advise young people embarking on their careers to choose their first job for its potential to teach them, rather than for the salary on offer; the same applies to whom they will work with, as well as the work itself.

Building a diverse professional network can be a game-changer. It opens doors to new opportunities, offers insights from various perspectives, and provides support when challenges arise. Imagine your network as a vibrant tapestry, woven with individuals from different industries and backgrounds. Each thread adds strength and colour to your professional life. Attending industry events and conferences is one way to start weaving this tapestry. These gatherings are not only about what you learn but who you meet. They offer a chance to engage with others who share your interests and goals. When attending such events, approach them with curiosity and openness. Listen more than you speak, ask questions, and remember that genuine interest often leads to meaningful connections.

Most successful business owners attribute a significant part of their success to the people they associate with. Jim Rohn, motivational speaker and business mentor, said, "You are the average of the five people you spend the most time with." Your income is also likely to be shaped by the people and environment you surround yourself with.

Seeking out Mastermind groups of entrepreneurs and business owners can, therefore, be the quickest way to connect with like-minded and supportive individuals who are already experienced in the domain you are about to enter. For many years, I have been involved with Vistage, a peer-to-peer advisory board, the Cranfield BGP Business Club programme, industry-specific mastermind clubs, and I have created my own Executive Supper Club as a means of bringing together like-minded business people in an informal setting where members can feel comfortable enough to share their concerns in a safe environment.

Connecting with influencers in your field may initially feel daunting, but consider them as mentors waiting to guide you. These individuals can provide advice, share valuable experiences, and even unlock doors that once seemed closed. Start by engaging with their work, read their articles, comment on their posts, or share their insights with your network. This lays a strong foundation for interaction. When reaching out, be genuine and articulate why you admire their work and what you hope to learn. Remember, influencers are people too; they value sincere engagement over flattery.

Finding mentors can significantly influence your entrepreneurial journey. Mentors provide wisdom drawn from their experiences, assisting you in navigating the complexities of business with greater ease. Identifying a mentor starts with understanding what you seek. Are you looking for industry-specific advice, or do you require someone who excels in leadership? Knowing this helps narrow down potential mentors who align with your needs. Successful mentor-mentee relationships are built on mutual respect and open communication.

Consider the example of Mark Zuckerberg and Steve Jobs; their relationship was characterised by candid discussions and shared values that left a lasting impression on Zuckerberg's leadership style.

Effectively leveraging your network requires more than merely collecting business cards. It's about nurturing those connections into relationships that provide mutual benefit. Organise regular networking meet-ups, whether virtual coffee chats or in-person gatherings, where ideas can flow freely. These meet-ups foster collaboration and keep you connected to the pulse of your industry. Techniques for maintaining relationships include sending thoughtful follow-up messages or sharing relevant articles that remind you of a conversation. A simple gesture can reinforce your connection and keep communication lines open.

Reciprocity is the heartbeat of networking. Giving back to your network strengthens bonds and enhances your reputation as a valuable contact. Sharing industry knowledge, resources, or opportunities demonstrates generosity and fosters goodwill. Mentoring others is another powerful way to give back while reinforcing your understanding of key concepts. By guiding another individual, you solidify your own knowledge and make a positive contribution to the community.

As you build connections, remember that networking isn't transactional; it's relational. Focus on fostering genuine interactions rather than seeking immediate gains. Embrace the notion that what you give often returns in unexpected ways, enriching both your personal growth and professional pursuits.

By cultivating a diverse network, engaging with mentors, and fostering reciprocal relationships, you lay the groundwork for sustained success in business. Networking transcends being a mere strategy; it develops into an enriching aspect of your entrepreneurial journey, offering opportunities for learning, collaboration, and growth at every turn.

This chapter is not just about networking for business gain; it is about weaving a rich tapestry of human connections that support both personal and professional growth. Through thoughtful engagement with others, you can cultivate a network that not only propels your business forward but also enriches your life in immeasurable ways.

STAYING UPDATED WITH INDUSTRY TRENDS

In the ever-evolving landscape of business, maintaining an acute awareness of industry developments is akin to possessing a finely tuned radar system that detects subtle shifts and emerging opportunities before they become glaringly apparent. This vigilance can serve as your invaluable competitive edge. By subscribing to various industry-specific publications and newsletters, you can effortlessly adopt a strategic and well-informed approach, thus remaining intricately connected to the flow of constant developments. These publications deliver insights into new and emerging trends, technological break-throughs, and evolved consumer behaviours. Picture them as your personal daily briefing that offers a straightforward yet comprehensive examination of the intricate changes brewing within your industry, effectively breaking down complex trans-formations into digestible updates. By keeping up with these resources, you ensure that you are always attuned to the pulse of your industry.

Furthermore, engaging with professional associations and forums provides a vital platform for exchanging knowledge and experiences. These collaborative groups foster a vibrant commu-nity of discussions that enable members to share insights and learn from peers facing similar challenges across a diverse range of industry landscapes. By actively participating, you can gain various perspectives that greatly enhance your understanding and inform critical strategic decisions in a manner that is thor-ough and comprehensive.

DYNAMIC INTEGRATION OF TRENDS

Incorporating industry trends into your business strategy is crucial for ensuring that you remain relevant and competitive. Treat this as a dynamic, ongoing process that involves constant analysis and forecasting of trends to anticipate changes effec-tively before they affect you. Utilising techniques such as PEST analysis (evaluating Political, Economic, Social, and Technolog-ical factors) can be highly beneficial for identifying external influences that might profoundly impact your domain. Once you've discerned potential trends, delve deeper into how these align with your strategic business goals and inherent capabilities. A prime example of this can be seen in Netflix's substantial pivot from DVD rentals to a focus on streaming services, a strategic transition that successfully capitalised on the burgeoning demand for easily accessible digital content and established its position as a front-runner in the ever-competitive entertainment industry. They identified the market trajectory and responded with strategic agility, showcasing the undeniable power of astute trend analysis in crafting strategic planning.

EMBRACING TECHNOLOGICAL ADVANCEMENTS

In this digital age, adapting to technological advancements is essential for maintaining operational efficiency and further enhancing service offerings. New technologies should be embraced not merely as tools but viewed as catalysts for transformative growth. Attending tech expos and innovation fairs enables you to witness firsthand how cutting-edge developments can seamlessly integrate into your existing business model. These dynamic events often showcase innovations that may initially seem futuristic but typically hold significant practical relevance for a broad range of industries. Consider how cloud computing revolutionised data management systems or how artificial intelligence (AI) is now reshaping customer service dynamics through the implementation of intuitive chatbots. Case studies of technology-driven transformations can offer invaluable lessons, such as Zara's strategic adoption of RFID technology for streamlined inventory management processes, which significantly bolstered efficiency and accuracy, serving as an explicit example of embracing technology to drive improved efficiencies.

NURTURING A CULTURE OF INNOVATION

Cultivating a culture that prioritises innovation involves establishing an environment where new and transformative ideas are not only welcomed but also actively explored and encouraged. Stimulate experimentation through innovation workshops and brainstorming sessions where employees feel emboldened to think beyond conventional boundaries without the fear of failure clouding their judgement. These sessions act as incubators for creative solutions, fostering a culture that thrives on novelty and exceptional adaptability. Instituting rewards for employees who contribute innovative ideas reinforces the inherent value placed on creativity, thus inspiring others to pursue bold and forward-thinking concepts. For instance, consider Google's "20% time" policy, which encourages employees to dedicate a portion of their workweek to engaging with passion projects unrelated to their prescribed responsibilities. This initiative has yielded remarkable innovations such as Gmail and Google News, showcasing the potential when a company fosters its spirit of innovation and creativity.

By incorporating these strategies into your business practices, you not only stay ahead of the curve but also foster an adaptive mindset within your organisation. In this era where industries evolve at unprecedented rates, remaining well-informed about developments shifts from being merely optional to an essential necessity. Let these practices guide your path in maintaining relevance amidst constant change, ensuring that your business preserves its agility, competitive position, and readiness to embrace new opportunities as they arise, prepared to seize the moment with wisdom and strategic foresight.

SETTING FUTURE GOALS FOR CONTINUOUS IMPROVEMENT

Crafting a roadmap for your business's future is akin to setting sail for a long voyage. The destination may be clear, but the winds will change and the currents will shift. Establishing a structured framework for goal-setting is essential to navigate these waters. One effective method is using OKRs (Objectives and Key Results), a system that aligns your goals with measurable outcomes. This approach ensures that everyone in your organisation moves in the same direction, focusing collective efforts on defined priorities. Imagine setting an objective like "Expand market share by 20%," with key results such as launching three new products and increasing customer retention by 15%. This clarity transforms ambitions into actionable targets.

Balancing long-term vision with short-term tactics is also essential. Long-term goals provide direction and purpose, establishing a foundation for growth over years or even decades. In contrast, short-term goals serve as stepping stones, enabling you to address immediate challenges and seize opportunities. They keep your team motivated by delivering quick wins, reinforcing the overarching vision. This dual approach ensures that while you pursue grand aspirations, you remain grounded in the present, making incremental progress towards realising your dreams.

Feedback plays a crucial role in refining and establishing meaningful goals. Gathering input from stakeholders, be they customers, employees, or partners, provides valuable insights that can reshape your objectives. Techniques such as surveys, focus groups, and one-on-one interviews reveal perceptions that may otherwise go unnoticed. This data serves as a compass, guiding adjustments to ensure goals remain relevant. Consider how feedback might underscore a need for more personalised customer service, prompting a shift in focus from expanding product lines to enhancing user experience. Such feedback-driven adjustments ensure that your goals align with real-world needs and expectations.

Tracking progress and celebrating milestones are essential for maintaining momentum and motivation. Goal-tracking software and tools like Trello or Asana provide real-time visibility into progress, assisting you in staying organised and accountable. They divide goals into manageable tasks, offering a quick overview of what has been accomplished and what lies ahead. Celebrating achievements, no matter how small, reinforces positive behaviour and sustains motivation. Recognition events or simple shout-outs during team meetings foster an atmosphere of encouragement and appreciation. These celebrations remind everyone of the impact their contributions have on the larger picture.

Regularly reviewing and adapting goals is essential to maintaining agility in a rapidly changing environment. Conducting quarterly goal reviews allows you to assess progress and pinpoint areas for improvement. These reviews are not merely about ticking off boxes; they provide opportunities to reflect on successes and setbacks, fostering a culture of continuous learning. Techniques for adjusting goals involve evaluating shifts in market dynamics or internal priorities. For example, if new competitors arise or consumer preferences change, it may be necessary to realign objectives to stay competitive. Embracing change ensures that you are not merely reacting but proactively guiding your business toward success.

In the grand tapestry of entrepreneurship, setting future goals serves as the threads weaving together vision, action, feedback, and adaptability. These elements create a resilient framework that propels your business forward while allowing flexibility to adapt to unforeseen challenges. As we conclude this chapter on continuous learning and adaptation, remember that the path of entrepreneurship is dynamic. Your goals are not set in stone; they are living elements that evolve with experience and insight.

BUSINESS IS A TEAM SPORT!

You've reached the end of the book. Congratulations!

Now you've got the tools to build something amazing. You know how to start your own business, become your own boss, and create your freedom. That's a big deal!

But there's one more way you can make a difference:

Share what you've found.

By leaving a quick, honest review of this book on Amazon, you can help other future business owners find the same advice, ideas, and inspiration you just got. It takes just a minute, but it could be the very thing someone else needs to take their first step.

This is how we keep the spirit of business alive—by passing on what we've learned and helping each other grow.

Click here to leave your review on Amazon:

[https://www.amazon.com/review/review-your-purchases/?asin=B0FC2T3D2N]

Thank you so much for your help. Your words can go a long way.

Stephen Brown

CONCLUSION

As we bring this journey to a close, let's take a moment to reflect on the transformative path of entrepreneurship we have travelled together. From the very first spark of an idea to the execution of a comprehensive business plan, this book has aimed to be your guide, your companion in the sometimes chaotic yet exhilarating world of starting a business.

We've explored the significance of establishing a solid foundation, a mindset strengthened by resilience, adaptability, and a readiness to embrace risk. These qualities are not merely desirable; they are essential for navigating the unpredictable waters of entrepreneurship.

Remember, every successful entrepreneur has confronted numerous challenges. What distinguishes them is their capability to learn from these experiences and persist in moving forward.

Planning, as we discussed, is not merely about writing a business plan. It involves setting a vision and mission that align with your core values, crafting SMART goals that serve as stepping stones, and employing tools like the Business Model Canvas to visualise and strategise effectively. These elements create a roadmap that guides you towards your objectives while allowing for flexibility and adaptation.

Throughout the book, practical tools, checklists, and processes are provided to empower you to better understand the three pillars of business: Sales, Finance, and Operations, and to apply these lessons directly to your business. Whether it's validating your business idea with real-world feedback or utilising digital marketing strategies, these tools support you at every step of your entrepreneurial journey.

We have also celebrated the success stories of individuals who, like you, set out with a dream and turned it into reality. These stories are not merely inspirational; they serve as proof that perseverance, strategic thinking, and a touch of grit can lead to remarkable achievements. Remember Sara Blakely and her journey with Spanx or the innovative path of Apple. These examples illustrate that success is achievable, but it demands dedication and hard work.

Now, I encourage you to reflect on your own aspirations. How can the knowledge and insights gained from this book shape your entrepreneurial journey? Take a moment to consider the steps you need to take, the challenges you may encounter, and the strategies you will use to overcome them.

This is your call to action. The time has come to take that first or next step in your venture. Use this book as your ongoing resource and guide. Refer back to the chapters, revisit the exercises, and draw upon the stories that resonate with you. Remember, the journey of entrepreneurship is not a sprint but a marathon. Pace yourself, remain focused, and keep moving forward.

As you move forward, remember that you are not alone. Take advantage of the learning opportunities and networking resources mentioned throughout this book. Connect with fellow entrepreneurs, seek mentorship, and cultivate a community of support and shared growth. There is strength in numbers, and together, we can achieve remarkable things.

Finally, let me reaffirm the vision we've shared—a vision of achieving freedom and prosperity through entrepreneurship. This vision is not only achievable; it is within your grasp. The world is awaiting your unique ideas and contributions. Embrace the challenges, celebrate the victories, and never lose sight of your dreams.

You are now equipped with the knowledge, tools, and motivation to embark on this exciting journey. Proceed with confidence and clarity. Your entrepreneurial adventure awaits, and I have no doubt you will make it a tremendous success.

GLOSSARY OF BUSINESS TERMS
A PRACTICAL GUIDE TO KEY TERMS FOR NEW BUSINESS OWNERS

Assets: Resources owned by a business that have value, such as cash, equipment, buildings, or inventory.

Balance Sheet: A financial statement showing a company's assets, liabilities, and equity.

Brand: The identity and perception of a business, including name, logo, reputation, and customer experience.

Break-even Point: The point at which a business's revenue exactly covers its costs.

Burn Rate: The rate at which a new business spends its capital before generating positive cash flow.

Business Model: How a company creates, delivers, and captures value, or how it generates revenue.

Cash Flow: The movement of money in and out of a business.

Corporation Tax: A tax your business pays on its profits.

CRM (Customer Relationship Management): Systems and strategies for managing a company's interactions with current and potential customers.

Crowdfunding: Raising small amounts of money from a large number of people, typically via online platforms, to fund a new venture.

Current Assets: Short-term assets expected to be converted into cash, sold, or consumed within one year. Examples include cash, inventory, and accounts receivable.

Current Liabilities: Obligations a business must settle within one year, including accounts payable, short-term loans, and accrued expenses.

Dividend: A portion of a limited company's profit paid out to its shareholders after corporation tax deduction.

EBITDA (Earnings Before Interest, Taxes, Depreciation, and Amortisation): A measure of a company's operating performance, often used to compare profitability without the impact of financial and accounting decisions.

Equity: Ownership in a business, referring to either the owner's stake or the shares issued to investors.

Fixed Assets: Long-term tangible assets used in the operations of a business, not expected to be converted into cash within a year. Examples include buildings, machinery, and vehicles.

Fixed Costs: Expenses that remain constant regardless of the level of production or sales, such as rent or base salaries.

Fixed Liabilities (also known as Long-term Liabilities): Debts or obligations not due within the next year. Examples include long-term loans, bonds payable, and lease obligations.

Gross Profit: Revenue minus the cost of goods sold (COGS). Does not include overhead expenses.

Insolvency: A business is considered insolvent when it lacks sufficient cash (cash flow insolvency) or its liabilities exceed its assets (balance sheet insolvency).

Invoice: A document sent to customers requesting payment for goods or services provided.

Kaizen: A Japanese term meaning "continuous improvement." It refers to a strategy where employees at all levels work together proactively to achieve regular, incremental improvements.

Kanban: A workflow management method that uses visual boards (physical or digital) to manage tasks and improve efficiency, commonly used in product development and project management.

Lean Startup: A methodology for developing businesses and products based on "build-measure-learn" cycles to validate ideas and reduce risk quickly.

Liabilities: The amount a business owes, including loans, accounts payable, and mortgages.

Liquidity: How easily your business can access cash to pay bills and handle day-to-day expenses.

Margin: The difference between the selling price of a product and its cost. Often expressed as a percentage.

Market Research: The process of gathering, analysing, and interpreting information about a market, including customers and competitors.

MVP (Minimum Viable Product): A version of a product with just enough features to satisfy early adopters and provide feedback for future development.

Net Profit: What remains from revenue/turnover after all expenses, taxes, and costs have been deducted. Also known as the "bottom line."

Operating Profit: The profit from your core business activities, before interest and tax.

Overheads: Ongoing costs, including rent, administration, and utilities. Also called indirect costs.

PESTEL: A strategic tool used to identify and analyse the external macro-environmental factors that can impact a business. The acronym stands for: **Political, Economic, Social, Technological, Environmental, Legal.**

Pitch: A presentation made to potential investors or partners explaining your business idea.

Pivot: A significant change in business strategy.

Profit: The financial gain a business makes: Revenue minus costs. It can be gross, operating or net depending on what's included in the costs.

Revenue (or Turnover): The total income generated from sales.

ROI (Return on Investment): A measure of the profitability of an investment, calculated as the gain or loss compared to the original cost.

Scalability: The ability of a business to grow and handle increased demand.

Seed Funding: Initial capital used to start a business.

SWOT Analysis: A planning tool used to identify a business's Strengths, Weaknesses, Opportunities, and Threats.

USP (Unique Selling Proposition): The feature or benefit that distinguishes your product or service from the competition.

Value Proposition: A clear statement explaining how your product solves customers' problems or improves their situation, and why it's better than alternatives.

Work in Progress (WIP): Partially completed goods or services not yet ready for sale.

Working Capital: The difference between a business's current assets and current liabilities.

REFERENCES

"Eat That Frog!" Brian Tracey (2001)

"Great by Choice," Jim Collins (2011)

10 Characteristics of Successful Entrepreneurs - HBS Online. Retrieved from https://online.hbs.edu/blog/post/characteristics-of-successful-entrepreneurs

Four Steps for Crafting Your Personal Mission Statement. Retrieved from https://www.smallbusiness.amazon/articles/four-steps-for-crafting-your-personal-mission-statement

5 Product Failures That Turned Out to Be Successes. Retrieved from https://clickup.com/blog/product-failures-turned-into-success/

Minimum Viable Product (MVP): What is it & Why it Matters. Retrieved from https://www.atlassian.com/agile/product-management/minimum-viable-product

The difference: Mission vs Vision Statements. Retrieved from https://www.atlassian.com/work-management/strategic-planning/mission-and-vision

5 Tips for Setting SMART Goals in Your Business Plan. Retrieved from https://www.business.com/articles/5-tips-for-setting-smart-business-goals/

5 Successful Business Model Canvas Examples. Retrieved from https://miro.com/strategic-planning/business-model-canvas-examples/

Financial Projections Template - SCORE. Retrieved from https://www.score.org/resource/template/financial-projections-template

Marketing Personas: Know Your Small Business Customers. Retrieved from https://masterful-marketing.com/marketing-personas-small-business-customers/

How to Use Facebook Audience Insights for Market Research. Retrieved from https://blog.woobox.com/2018/03/how-to-use-facebook-audience-insights-for-market-research/

SWOT Analysis: Examples and Templates [2025]. Retrieved from https://asana.com/resources/swot-analysis

A Complete Overview of the Best Data Visualization Tools. Retrieved from https://www.toptal.com/designers/data-visualization/data-visualization-tools

LLC vs. Corporation: Which Is Right for Your Business?. Retrieved from https://www.nerdwallet.com/article/small-business/llc-vs-corporation

Federal trademark searching: Getting started. Retrieved from https://www.uspto.gov/learning-and-resources/uspto-videos/federal-trademark-searching-getting-started-0

Every Tax Deadline You Need To Know - TurboTax - Intuit. Retrieved from https://turbotax.intuit.com/tax-tips/tax-planning-and-checklists/important-tax-deadlines-dates/L7Rn92V1d

How to Protect Your IP as a Startup | CO. Retrieved from https://www.uschamber.com/co/start/strategy/protecting-intellectual-property-for-startups

Companies That Succeeded With Bootstrapping. Retrieved from https://www.investopedia.com/articles/investing/082814/companies-succeeded-bootstrapping.asp

10 Best Crowdfunding Sites and Platforms in 2025 - Shopify. Retrieved from https://www.shopify.com/blog/crowdfunding-sites

How Do Angel Investors and Venture Capitalists Differ?. Retrieved from https://www.business.com/articles/angel-investors-vs-venture-capitalists

Loans | U.S. Small Business Administration. Retrieved from https://www.sba.gov/funding-programs/loans

14 Brand Identity Examples to Inspire Your Own. Retrieved from https://www.wix.com/blog/brand-identity-examples

16 Effective Marketing Strategies To Boost Sales In 2023. Retrieved from https://www.forbes.com/councils/forbescommunicationscouncil/2022/12/19/16-effective-marketing-strategies-to-boost-sales-in-2023/

5 Best Social Media Platforms for Marketing and Advertising. Retrieved from https://clictadigital.com/5-best-social-media-platforms-for-marketing-and-advertising/

Developing a Content Marketing Strategy. Retrieved from https://contentmarketinginstitute.com/developing-a-strategy/

Writing an Effective Job Description | Human Resources. Retrieved from https://www.wright.edu/human-resources/writing-an-effective-job-description

Starting and Maintaining a Diversity Recruitment Strategy. Retrieved from https://www.indeed.com/hire/c/info/diversity-recruiting-strategy

Behavioral Interviewing: Definition & 42 Sample Questions. Retrieved from https://eddy.com/hr-encyclopedia/behavioral-interviewing/

How Leaders Build Trust. Retrieved from https://www.harvardbusiness.org/good-leadership-it-all-starts-with-trust/

Marketing Conversion Funnels from Top Companies in 2023. Retrieved from https://maven.com/articles/marketing-funnel

9 Guiding Principles for Doing Startup Customer Service Well. Retrieved from https://www.helpscout.com/helpu/5-customer-service-tips-for-startups/

Designing a successful loyalty program strategy. Retrieved from https://www.openloyalty.io/insider/designing-a-loyalty-program-strategy-phil-hussey

Customer Feedback Strategy: The Only Guide You'll Ever ... Retrieved from https://www.hubspot.com/customer-feedback

Top 10 process mapping tools in 2024. Retrieved from https://www.qntrl.com/blog/process-mapping-tools.html

Lean Thinking and Methods - Kaizen | US EPA. Retrieved from https://www.epa.gov/sustainability/lean-thinking-and-methods-kaizen

8 Top Business Automation Tools to Use in 2023. Retrieved from https://automateddreams.com/blog/8-top-business-automation-tools-to-use-in-2023/

Building Scalable Business Models. Retrieved from https://sloanreview.mit.edu/article/building-scalable-business-models/

Choosing the Best Risk Management Framework for Small ... Retrieved from https://bawn.com/risk-resilience-bawns-guide-to-cybersecurity-and-beyond/choosing-the-best-risk-management-framework-for-small-businesses

5 Real-World Project Risk Management Case Studies You ... Retrieved from https://www.intelegain.com/5-real-world-project-risk-management-case-studies-you-should-know/

Success Through Adaptive Leadership: Principles To ... Retrieved from https://www.forbes.com/councils/forbesbusinesscouncil/2023/08/31/success-through-adaptive-leadership-principles-to-cultivate/

Creating an innovation culture. Retrieved from https://www.mckinsey.com/capabilities/strategy-and-corporate-finance/our-insights/creating-an-innovation-culture

Characteristics Of A Scalable Business Model. Retrieved from https://www.leangroup.com/blog/the-importance-of-scalability-for-business-development

Five Technology Tools for Scalability in Business. Retrieved from https://www.leangroup.com/blog/five-technology-tools-for-scalability-in-business

How strategic partnering can fuel better business growth. Retrieved from https://www.simon-kucher.com/en/insights/how-strategic-partnering-can-fuel-better-business-growth

How to scale a business: Key challenges and solutions. Retrieved from https://www.hudsonoutsourcing.com/en_us/how-to-scale-a-business-key-challenges-and-solutions/

Understanding Growth Mindset vs Fixed Mindset - Mentorloop. Retrieved from https://mentorloop.com/blog/growth-mindset-vs-fixed-mindset-what-do-they-really-mean/

Power of Connections: Networking Strategies for Entrepreneurs. Retrieved from https://gsep.pepperdine.edu/blog/posts/power-of-connections-networking-strategies-for-entrepreneurs.htm

The Importance Of Staying Current With Industry Trends. Retrieved from https://sertifier.com/blog/staying-current-with-industry-trends/

A Guide to Setting Effective Entrepreneur Goals. Retrieved from https://meridianuniversity.edu/content/a-guide-to-setting-effective-entrepreneur-goals

Visi Misi Value Archives - Duage Management. Retrieved from https://duage.id/blog/tag/visi-misi-value/

APEX Intellectual Property Group | Trademark Prosecution. Retrieved from https://apexipgroup.com/trademark-prosecution/

The Power of Crowdfunding: Turning Ideas into Reality | Doctor Eya News. Retrieved from https://doctoreyanews.com/24683-the-power-of-crowdfunding-turning-ideas-into-reality-52/

Best Practices For Designing Effective Landing Pages - G-FX.net. Retrieved from https://g-fx.net/best-practices-for-designing-effective-landing-pages/

10 Best Time Management Strategies. Retrieved from https://assist-o.com/time-management-strategies/

How to Create an Effective Risk Management Plan - European Business Review. Retrieved from https://www.europeanbusinessreview.co.uk/how-to-create-an-effective-risk-management-plan/

INTRODUCTION TO USING FINANCIAL RATIOS FOR STOCK ANALYSIS | NSM News. Retrieved from https://nsmnews.com/threads/introduction-to-using-financial-ratios-for-stock-analysis.18007/

Key Financial Metrics to Drive Business Success and Sustainability - Business Probe. Retrieved from https://businessprobe.com/metrics-to-drive-business-success/

Hamed, R. (2023). The Role of Internal Control Systems in Ensuring Financial Performance Sustainability. Sustainability, 15(13), 10206.

Guide to All Financial Ratios. Retrieved from https://www.jaroeducation.com/blog/guide-to-financial-ratio/

Debt Ratio: Explanation and how to calculate it | Swoop. Retrieved from https://swoopfunding.com/uk/business-glossary/debt-ratio/

Debt To Enterprise Value Ratio Calculator - Savvy Calculator. Retrieved from https://savvycalculator.com/debt-to-enterprise-value-ratio-calculator/

Adient PLC (ADNT) | Solvency ratios. Retrieved from https://stock-data.online/stock/adnt/solvency-ratio

ABOUT THE AUTHOR

Stephen Brown is the Founder and Managing Director of Euro Projects Recruitment. This specialist consultancy has supported the growth of hundreds of businesses in the UK, USA and across Europe by helping them attract and retain exceptional technical, commercial, and executive talent. With more than 30 years of experience working at the intersection of people, performance, and strategy, Stephen has become a trusted advisor to entrepreneurs and leadership teams looking to scale their organisations in sustainable, practical ways.

Stephen's depth of business acumen is rooted in his hands-on experience of working closely with SME owners across a diverse range of sectors, from advanced engineering and manufacturing to professional services and high-growth startups. His insights span far beyond recruitment, covering the full spectrum of business building: strategic planning, leadership development, marketing, operational execution, and organisational culture.

A graduate of the esteemed Cranfield Business Growth Programme (BGP), one of the UK's most respected courses for ambitious SME leaders, Stephen merges contemporary academic theory with practical, front-line business experience. A strong belief in continuous learning informs his approach, highlighting the power of strategic clarity and the necessity of aligning people with purpose.

In addition to his business accomplishments, Stephen is also a passionate philanthropist and active fundraiser. He has spearheaded numerous initiatives to raise funds for UNICEF, engaging his professional network to support vulnerable children worldwide. His ability to merge business with social impact reflects his broader commitment to purposeful entrepreneurship.

In *"Start and Build a Successful Business"*, Stephen distils decades of experience into a clear, honest, and actionable guide. Whether you are launching your first business or scaling an existing one, this book offers practical tools, insights, and encouragement to help you create a strong, resilient, and rewarding enterprise.

Printed in Dunstable, United Kingdom

75404616R00112